Correlation Analysis of Stock Indices:
A Proportional Study

Dr. B. Ravi Kumar
Dr. Ch. Rama Krishna

CANADIAN
Academic Publishing

2015

Price : $27.86

First Edition : 2015

ISBN : 978-1-926488-05-9

Publisher ISBN Prefix : 978-1-926488

ISBN Allotment Agency : Library and Archives Canada (Govt. of Canada)

Published & Printed by
Canadian Academic Publishing
81, Woodlot Crescent,
Etobicoke,
Toronto, Ontario, Canada.
Postal Code- M9W 6T3
Phone- +1 (647) 633 9712
http://www.canadapublish.com

ABOUT THE BOOK

In order to understand the international transmission mechanism between the two markets under consideration, first it is important to recognize that the NSE and NASDAQ markets do not have any overlapping trading hours. There is a time lag of twelve-and-half hours between US Eastern Standard Time and Indian Standard Time.

The trading hours of both the markets are shown in below. In Indian Standard Time (IST), NSE opens at 10.00 AM and closes at 3.30 PM. In the modern world the size of the investors has been increased enormously and it is important to analyse the pattern of returns on stock indices for investment. The present research work is a comparative study on returns of NSE along with NASDAQ.

CONTENTS

CONTENTS

CONTENTS

CHAPTER – I

INTRODUCTION

1. 1   INTRODUCTION

Many factors, such as enterprise performance, dividends, stock prices of other countries, gross domestic product, exchange rates, interest rates, current account, money supply, employment, their information etc. have an impact on daily stock prices (Kurihara, 2006: p.376).The issue of inter temporal relation between stock returns and exchange rates has recently preoccupied the minds of economists, for theoretical and empirical reasons, since they both play important roles in influencing the development of a country's economy. In addition, the relationship between stock returns and foreign exchange rates has frequently been utilized in predicting the future trends for each other by investors. Moreover, the continuing increases in the world trade and capital movements have made the exchange rates as one of the main determinants of business profitability and equity prices (Kim, 2003). Exchange rate changes directly influence the international competitiveness of firms, given their impact on input and output price (Joseph, 2002). Basically, foreign exchange rate volatility influences the value of the firm since the future cash flows of the firm change with the fluctuations in the foreign exchange rates. When the Exchange rate appreciates, since exporters will lose their competitiveness in international market, the sales and profits of exporters will shrink and the stock prices will decline. On the other hand, importers will increase their competitiveness in domestic markets. Therefore, their profit and stock prices will increase. The depreciation of exchange rate will make adverse effects on exporters and importers. Exporters will have advantage against other countries' exporters and increase their sales and their stock prices will be higher (Yau and Nieh, 2006). That is, currency appreciation has both a negative and a positive effect on the domestic stock market for an export-dominant and an import-dominated country, respectively (Ma and Kao, 1990). Exchange rates can affect stock prices not only for multinational and export-oriented firms but also for domestic firms. For a multinational company, changes in exchange rates will result in an immediate change in value of its foreign operations as well as a continuing change in the profitability of its foreign operations reflected in successive income statements. Therefore, the changes in economic value of firm's foreign operations may influence stock prices. Domestic firms can also be influenced by changes in exchange rates since they may import a part of their inputs and export their outputs. For example, a devaluation of its currency makes imported inputs more expensive and exported outputs cheaper for a firm. Thus, devaluation will make positive effect for export firms (Agarwal, 1981) and increase the income of these firms, consequently, boosting the average level of stock prices (Wu, 2000). Thus, understanding this relationship will help domestic as well as international investors

1

for hedging and diversifying their portfolio. Also, fundamentalist investors have taken into account these relationships to predict the future trends for each other (Phylaktis and Ravazzolo, 2005; Mishra et al., 2007; Nieh and Lee, 2001; Stavarek, 2005).

Globalization and financial sector reforms in India have ushered in a sea change in the financial architecture of the economy. In the contemporary scenario, the activities in the financial markets and their relationships with the real sector have assumed significant importance. Since the inception of the financial sector reforms in the beginning of 1990's, the implementation of various reform measures have brought in a dramatic change in the functioning of the financial sector of the economy. Floating exchange rate that has been implemented in India since 1991, facilitates greater volume of trade and high volatility in equity as well as Forex market, increasing its exposure to economic and financial risks. The relationship between the two financial variables-stock returns and exchange rates- became especially significant in the wake of the 1997 economic crisis in Asian countries, which caused stock prices and exchange rate to fall across Asian markets. It has been suggested that difference in expected stock returns should be related to changes in exchange rates. Moreover, in the recent years, because of increasing international diversification, cross-market return correlations, gradual abolishment of capital inflow barriers and foreign exchange restrictions or the adoption of more flexible exchange rate arrangements in emerging and transition countries, these two markets have become significantly interdependent. These changes have increased the variety of investment opportunities as well as the volatility of exchange rates and risk of investment decisions and portfolio diversification process. Altogether, the whole gamut of institutional reforms concomitant to globalization programme, introduction of new instruments, change in procedures, widening of network of participants call for a re-examination of the relationship between the stock market and the foreign sector of India. Correspondingly, researches are also being conducted to understand the current working of the economic and the financial system in the new scenario. Interesting results are emerging particularly for the developing countries where the markets are experiencing new relationships which are not perceived earlier. Although, economic theory suggests that foreign exchange changes can have an important impact on the stock price by affecting cash flow, investment and profitability of firms, there is no consensus about these relationship and the empirical studies of the relationship are inconclusive (Joseph, 2002; Vygodina, 2006).

1.2   OVERVIEW OF THE MARKET

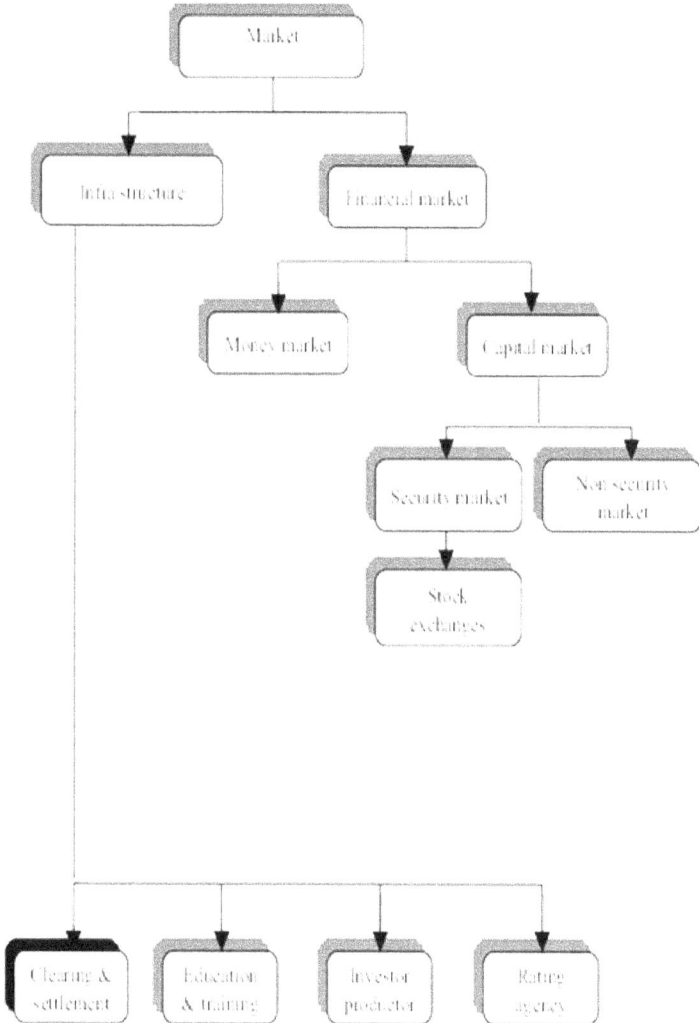

Fig 1.1 Overview of the market

1.3 FINANCIAL MARKET

A **financial market** is a market in which people and entities can trade financial securities, commodities, and other fungible items of value at low transaction costs and at prices that reflect supply and demand. Securities include stocks and bonds, and commodities include precious metals or agricultural goods.

There are both general markets (where many commodities are traded) and specialized markets (where only one commodity is traded). Markets work by placing many interested buyers and sellers, including households, firms, and government agencies, in one "place", thus making it easier for them to find each other. An economy which relies primarily on interactions between buyers and sellers to allocate resources is known as a market economy in contrast either to a command economy or to a non-market economy such as a gift economy.

In finance, financial markets facilitate:
- The raising of capital (in the capital markets)
- The transfer of risk (in the derivatives markets)
- Price discovery
- Global transactions with integration of financial markets
- The transfer of liquidity (in the money markets)
- International trade (in the currency markets)

– and are used to match those who want capital to those who have it.

Typically a borrower issues a receipt to the lender promising to pay back the capital. These receipts are securities which may be freely bought or sold. In return for lending money to the borrower, the lender will expect some compensation in the form of interest or dividends. This return on investment is a necessary part of markets to ensure that funds are supplied to them.

1.3.1 TYPES OF FINANCIAL MARKETS

Within the financial sector, the term "financial markets" is often used to refer just to the markets that are used to raise finance: for long term finance, the Capital markets; for short term finance, the Money markets. Another common use of the term is as a catchall for all the markets in the financial sector, as per examples in the breakdown below.

- Capital markets which consist of:
- Stock markets, which provide financing through the issuance of shares or common stock, and enable the subsequent trading thereof.
- Bond markets, which provide financing through the issuance of bonds, and enable the subsequent trading thereof.
- Commodity markets, which facilitate the trading of commodities.
- Money markets, which provide short term debt financing and investment.

- Derivatives markets, which provide instruments for the management of financial risk.
- Futures markets, which provide standardized forward contracts for trading products at some future date; see also forward market.
- Insurance markets, which facilitate the redistribution of various risks.
- Foreign exchange markets, which facilitate the trading of foreign exchange.

1.3.2 MONEY MARKETS

As money became a commodity, the **money market** became a component of the financial markets for assets involved in short-term borrowing, lending, buying and selling with original maturities of one year or less. Trading in the money markets is done over the counter, is wholesale. Various instruments exist, such as Treasury bills, commercial paper, bankers' acceptances, deposits, certificates of deposit, bills of exchange, repurchase agreements, federal funds, and short-lived mortgage-, and asset-backed securities. It provides liquidity funding for the global financial system. Money markets and capital markets are parts of financial markets. The instruments bear differing maturities, currencies, credit risks, and structure. Therefore they may be used to distribute the exposure.

1.3.3 CAPITAL MARKETS

Capital markets provide for the buying and selling of long term debt or equity backed securities. When they work well, the capital markets channel the wealth of savers to those who can put it to long term productive use, such as companies or governments making long term investments.

A key division within the capital markets is between the primary markets and secondary markets. In primary markets, new stock or bond issues are sold to investors, often via a mechanism known as underwriting. The main entities seeking to raise long term funds on the primary capital markets are governments (which may be municipal, local or national) and business enterprises (companies). Governments tend to issue only bonds, whereas companies often issue either equity or bonds. The main entities purchasing the bonds or stock include pension funds, hedge funds, sovereign wealth funds, and less commonly wealthy individuals and investment banks trading on their own behalf. In the secondary markets, existing securities are sold and bought among investors or traders, usually on a securities exchange, over-the-counter, or elsewhere. The existence of secondary markets increases the willingness of investors in primary markets, as they know they are likely to be able to swiftly cash out their investments if the need arises.

A second important division falls between the stock markets (for equity securities, also known as shares, where investors acquire ownership of companies) and the bond markets (where investors become creditors).

1.4   STOCK EXCHANGE

The stock exchange is the important segment of its capital market. If the stock exchange is well-regulated function smoothly, then it is an indicator of healthy capital market. If the state of the stock exchange is good, the overall capital market will grow and otherwise it can suffer a great set back which is not good for the country. The government at various stages controls the stock market and the capitals market.

A capital market deals in financial assets, excluding coin and currency. Banking accounts compromises the majority of financial assets. Pension and provident funds insurance policies shares and securities. Financial assets are claim of holders over issuer (business firms and governments). They enter low different segment of financial market. Those having short maturities that are non transferable like bank savings and current accounts set the identification of the monetary financial assets. This market is known as money market, Equity, Preferential shares and bonds and debentures issued by companies and securities issued by the government constitute the financial assets, which are traded in the capital market.

Both money market and capital market constitute the financial market. Capital market generally known as stock exchange. This is a institution around which every activity of national capital market revolves. Through the medium stock exchange the investor gets on impetus and motivations to invest in securities without which they would not be able to liquidate the securities. If there would have been no stock exchange many of the savers would have hold their saving either in cash i.e. idle or in bank with low interest rate or low returns. The stock exchange provides the opportunity to investors for the continuous trading in securities. It is continuously engaged in the capital mobilization process.

Another consequence of non-existence of stock exchange would have been low saving of the community, which means low investment and lower development of the country.

S	-	Securities provide for investor.
T	-	Tax Benefits planning and exemption.
O	-	Optimum return on investment.
C	-	Cautious Approach.
K	-	Knowledge of Market.
Ex	-	Exchange of Securities Transacted.
C	-	Cyclopedia of Listed Companies.
H	-	High Yield.
A	-	Authentic Information
N	-	New Entrepreneur encouraged.
G	-	Guidance of Investor & Company.
E	-	Equity

1.5   INDIAN STOCK MARKET

1.5.1   INTRODUCTION

Indian Stock Markets is one of the oldest in Asia. Its history dates back to nearly 200 years ago. The earliest records of security dealings in India are meager and obscure. **The East India Company** was the dominant institution in those days and business in its loan securities used to be transacted towards the close of the eighteenth century.

By 1830's business on corporate stocks and shares in Bank and Cotton presses took place in Bombay. Though the trading list was broader in 1839, there were only half a dozen brokers recognized by banks and merchants during 1840 and 1850. The 1850's witnessed a rapid development of commercial enterprise and brokerage business attracted many men into the field and by 1860 the number of brokers increased into 60. In 1860-61 the American Civil War broke out and cotton supply from United States to Europe was stopped; thus, the **'Share Mania'** in India began. The number of brokers increased to about 200 to 250.

At the end of the American Civil War, the brokers who thrived out of Civil War in 1874, found a place in a street (now appropriately called as Dalal Street) where they would conveniently assemble and transact business. In 1887, they formally established in Bombay, the **"Native Share and Stock Brokers' Association"**, which is alternatively known as **"The Stock Exchange"**. In 1895, the Stock Exchange acquired a premise in the same street and it was inaugurated in 1899. Thus, the Stock Exchange at Bombay was consolidated.

The Indian stock market has been assigned an important place in financing the Indian corporate sector. The principal functions of the stock markets are:
- enabling mobilizing resources for investment directly from the investors
- providing liquidity for the investors and monitoring.
- Disciplining company management.

The two major stock exchanges in India are
  ➢ **National Stock Exchange** (NSE)
  ➢ **Bombay Stock Exchange** (BSE).

1.5.2 NATIONAL STOCK EXCHANGE

With the liberalization of the Indian economy, it was found inevitable to lift the Indian stock market trading system on par with the international standards. On the basis of the recommendations of high powered Pherwani Committee. The National Stock Exchange was incorporated in 1992 by Industrial Development Bank of India, Industrial Credit and Investment Corporation of India, Industrial Finance Corporation of India, all Insurance Corporations, selected commercial banks and others.

The **National Stock Exchange** (NSE) is India's leading stock exchange covering various cities and towns across the country. NSE was set up by leading institutions to provide a modern, fully automated screen-based trading system with national reach. The Exchange has brought about unparalleled transparency, speed & efficiency, safety and market integrity. It has set up facilities that serve as a model for the securities industry in terms of **systems**, **practices** and **procedures.**

Trading at NSE can be classified under two broad categories:
- **Wholesale debt market**
- **Capital market**

Wholesale debt market operations are similar to money market operations - institutions and corporate bodies enter into high value transactions in financial instruments such as government securities, treasury bills, public sector unit bonds, commercial paper, certificate of deposit, etc.

Capital market: A market where debt or equity securities are traded.

There are two kinds of players in NSE:
- Trading members
- Participants

Recognized members of NSE are called trading members who trade on behalf of themselves and their clients. Participants include trading members and large players like banks who take direct settlement responsibility.

Trading at NSE takes place through a fully automated screen-based trading mechanism which adopts the principle of an order-driven market. Trading members can stay at their offices and execute the trading, since they are linked through a communication network.

The prices at which the buyer and seller are willing to transact will appear on the screen. When the prices match the transaction will be completed and a confirmation slip will be printed at the office of the trading member.

NSE has several advantages over the traditional trading exchanges. They are as follows:
- NSE brings an integrated stock market trading network across the nation.
- Investors can trade at the same price from anywhere in the country since inter-market operations are streamlined coupled with the countrywide access to the securities.
- Delays in communication, late payments and the malpractice's prevailing in the traditional trading mechanism can be done away with greater operational efficiency and informational transparency in the stock market operations, with the support of total computerized network.

1.5.3 NSE NIFTY

S&P CNX Nifty is a **well-diversified 50 stock index** accounting for 22 sectors of the economy. It is used for a variety of purposes such as benchmarking fund portfolios, index based derivatives and index funds.

NSE came to be owned and managed by India Index Services and Products Ltd. (IISL), which is a joint venture between NSE and CRISIL. IISL is India's first specialized company focused upon the index as a core product. IISL have a consulting and licensing agreement with Standard & Poor's (S&P), who are world leaders in index services. CNX stands for CRISIL NSE Indices. CNX ensures common branding of indices, to reflect the identities of both the promoters, i.e. NSE and CRISIL. Thus, 'C' Stands for CRISIL, 'N' stands for NSE and X stands for Exchange or Index. The S&P prefix belongs to the US-based Standard & Poor's Financial Information Services.

1.5.4 BOMBAY STOCK EXCHANGE

The Bombay Stock Exchange is one of the oldest stock exchanges in Asia. It was established as **"The Native Share & Stock Brokers Association"** in 1875. It is the first stock exchange in the country to obtain permanent recognition in 1956 from the Government of India under the Securities Contracts (Regulation) Act, 1956. The Exchange's pivotal and pre-eminent role in the development of the Indian capital market is widely recognized and its index, **SENSEX,** is tracked worldwide.

1.5.5 SENSEX

The Stock Exchange, Mumbai (BSE) in 1986 came out with a stock index that subsequently became the barometer of the Indian stock market.

SENSEX is not only scientifically designed but also based on globally accepted construction and review methodology. First compiled in 1986, SENSEX is a **basket of 30 constituent stocks** representing a sample of large, liquid and representative companies. The base year of SENSEX is 1978-79 and the base value is 100. The index is widely reported in both domestic and international markets through print as well as electronic media.

Due to is wide acceptance amongst the Indian investors; SENSEX is regarded to be the pulse of the Indian stock market. As the oldest index in the country, it provides the time series data over a fairly long period of time. Small wonder, the SENSEX has over the years become one of the most prominent brands in the country.

The SENSEX captured all these events in the most judicial manner. One can identify the booms and busts of the Indian stock market through SENSEX.

The launch of SENSEX in 1986 was later followed up in January 1989 by introduction of BSE National Index (Base: 1983-84 = 100). It comprised of 100 stocks listed at five major stock exchanges. The values of all BSE indices are updated every 15 seconds during the market hours and displayed through the BOLT system, BSE website and news wire agencies.

All BSE-indices are reviewed periodically by the "index committee" of the exchange.

1.6 OVERVIEW OF THE REGULATORY FRAMEWORK OF THE CAPITAL MARKET IN INDIA

India has a financial system that is regulated by independent regulators in the sectors of banking, insurance, capital markets and various service sectors. The Indian Financial system is regulated by two governing agencies under the Ministry of Finance. They are

1. **Reserve Bank of India**
   The RBI was set up in 1935 and is the central bank of India. It regulates the financial and banking system. It formulates monetary policies and prescribes exchange control norms.

2. **The Securities Exchange Board of India**
   The Government of India constituted SEBI on April 12, 1988, as a non-statutory body to promote orderly and healthy development of the securities market and to provide investor protection.

1.6.1 DEPARTMENT OF ECONOMIC AFFAIRS

The capital markets division of the Department of Economic Affairs regulates capital markets and securities transactions. The capital markets division has been entrusted with the responsibility of assisting the Government in framing suitable policies for the orderly growth and development of the securities markets with the SEBI, RBI and other agencies. It is also responsible for the functioning of the Unit Trust of India (UTI) and Securities and Exchange Board of India (SEBI).

The principal aspects that are dealt with the capital market division are:

- Policy matters relating to the securities market
- Policy matters relating to the regulation and development and investor protection of the securities market and the debt market.
- Organizational and operational matters relating to SEBI

The Capital Market is governed by:

- Securities Contract (Regulation) Act, 1956
- Securities Contract (Regulation) Rules, 1957
- SEBI Act, 1992
- Companies Act 1956
- SEBI (Stock Brokers and Sub Brokers) Rules, 1992
- Exchange Bye-Laws Rules & Regulations

1.6.2 SELF-REGULATING ROLE OF THE EXCHANGE

The exchange functions as a Self Regulatory Organization with the parameters laid down by the SCRA, SEBI Act, SEBI Guidelines and Rules, Bye-laws and Regulations of the Exchange. The Governing Board discharges these functions. The Executive Director has all the powers of the governing board except discharging a member indefinitely or declaring him a defaulter or expelling him. The Executive Director takes decisions in the areas like surveillance, inspection, investigation, etc. in an objective manner as per the parameters laid down by the governing board or the statutory committees like the Disciplinary Action Committee.

1.7   TRADING WITH STOCK MARKET

Trading: It is a process by which a customer is given facility to buy and sell share this buying and selling can only be done through some broker and this is where Arcadia helps its customer. A customer willing to trade with any brokerage house need to have a demat account, trading account and saving account with a brokerage firm. Any one having following document can open all the above mentioned account and can start trading.

1.7.1 BASIC REQUIREMENT FOR DOING TRADING

Trading requires Opening a Demat account. Demat refers to a dematerialized account. We need to open a Demat account if we want to buy or sell stocks. So it is just like a bank account where actual money is replaced by shares. We need to approach the Depository Participants (DP, they are like bank branches), to open Demat account. A **depository** is a place where the stocks of investors are held in electronic form. The depository has agents who are called **depository participants** (DPs).

1.7.2 TRADING METHOD

Listing securities are traded on the floor of recognized stock exchange where its member traded. An investor is not permitted to enter the floor of stock exchange and he has trust the broker to:
- Negotiate the best price for the trade.
- Settle the account, i.e. payment for securities sold on due date.
- Take delivery of securities purchase.

1.7.3 TYPES OF TRADING
Trading in stock exchange is conducted in two ways:
- Ready delivery contract.
- Forward delivery contract.

1.7.4 BASKET TRADING SYSTEM

The Basket Trading System provides the arbitrageurs an opportunity to take advantage of price differences in the underlying Sensex and Futures on the Sensex by simultaneous buying and selling of baskets comprising the Sensex scrips in the Cash Segment and Sensex Futures. This is expected to provide balancing impact on the prices in both cash and futures markets.

The Exchange has commenced trading in the Derivatives Segment with effect from June 9, 2000 to enable the investors to, inter-alias, hedge their risks. Initially, the facility of trading in the Derivatives Segment was confined to Index Futures. Subsequently, the Exchange has introduced the Index Options and Options & Futures in select individual stocks. The investors in cash market had felt a need to limit their risk exposure in the market to movement in Sensex.

To participate in this system, the member-brokers need to indicate number of Sensex basket(s) to be bought or sold, where the value of one Sensex basket is arrived at by the system by multiplying Rs.50 to prevailing Sensex. For e.g., if the Sensex is 4000, then value of one basket of Sensex would be 4000 x 50= i.e., Rs. 2,00,000/-. The investors can also place orders by entering value of Sensex portfolio to be brought or sold with a minimum value of Rs. 50,000/- for each order.

1.7.5 PROCEDURE OF TRADING

1.   Select of broker
The first step is buying or selling of share is to select a broker for transaction business on behalf of the investor. The trading of securities on the stock exchange can be done through members of the exchange.
- An investor prefers to select a broker who shall.
- Act with due skill. Care and diligence in the conduct of all his business.
- Not create false market either singly or in concert with other.

2.   Opening an Account With The Broker
The next step to open account with the broker. It helps the investor to provide his credit worthiness, if the clients were not to do margin money with the broker.

3.   Selection of Securities
This is application for buying securities. The investor may be consulted with broker and take advise for selection of securities.

4.   Selection of Time for Trading
This is important to get the best advantage from buying or selling the securities.

5.   Placing an Order
Various method of placing an order with the broker has been evolved to give the broker leverage when he is on the floor of the stock exchange.

6.   Preparation of Contract Note
SEBI circular of 4th Feb. 1991 requires that all member of the recognized stock exchange issue contract note to the investors on the execution of trade. Brokers, therefore issue contract note to the client, which gives the name of the company, price of trade, brokerage, time of execution, provision regarding arbitration etc. in term of the bye-laws of stock exchange, this is statutory requirement and mandatory.

7.   Settlement
The settlement is the process whereby payment is made by brokers who have made purchase and share delivery by those brokers who have made sales.

Techniques and Instruments for Trading
The various techniques that are available in the hands of a client are:-
1.   Delivery
2.   Intraday
3.   Future
4.   Forwards
5.   Options
6.   swaps

1.8 FUNCTIONS OF A STOCK EXCHANGES

The role of a stock exchange in a capital market is as follows:-

1) Ready and Continuous Market: The stock exchange provides a ready and continuous market for the sale and purchase of securities.

2) Bank Borrowing Facility: Securities listed on a stock exchange serve as a collateral security when an investor need funds from a bank.

3) Promotes Capital Formation: Stock Exchanges promotes capital formation as they encourage investors to invest need funds from a bank.

4) Safety and Fair Dealing: The Stock Exchange operates under rules and regulations framed by the Central Government. The rules and regulations framed by the Central Government are in the interest to ensure safety to the investors and whatever be their dealings, it should a fair one.

5) Government Funding: Stock Exchanges helps the government to raise funds by selling shares and debentures.

6) Creation of Employment Opportunities: Stock Exchange creates a number of employment opportunities to a number of brokers, sub brokers as they are the intermediaries through which shares are being sold.

7) Evaluation of Securities: Stock Exchanges helps to evaluate the worth of securities, as securities are traded at a certain price on the stock market. Investors are able to determine the real worth of their holdings in the form of shares and debentures which are listed on the stock exchange.

8) Industrial Development: The capital collected through shares and debentures can be put to industrial use. With the capital, new industries can be started, existing ones can be expanded and modernized and thereby enhancing the industrial development of a country.

9) Clearing House of Securities: The Stock Exchanges acts as a clearing house of securities. It facilitates easy and quick clearance of transactions of securities between the buyers and the sellers.

10) Facilitates Flow of Capital: Stock Exchange facilitate the flow of capital to companies who have a high potential to raise substantial funds.

CHAPTER – II

OBJECTIVES, METHODOLOGY & LITERATURE REVIEW

2.1 RATIONALE AND SCOPE OF THE STUDY

The Indian stock market though one of the oldest in Asia being in operation since 1875, remained largely outside the global integration process until the late 1980s. A number of developing countries in concert with the International Finance Corporation and the World Bank took steps in the 1980s to establish and revitalize their stock markets as an effective way of mobilizing and allocation of finance. In line with the global trend, reform of the Indian stock market began with the establishment of Securities and Exchange Board of India in 1988. However the reform process gained momentum only in the aftermath of the external payments crisis of 1991 followed by the securities scam of 1992. Among the significant measures of integration, portfolio investment by FIIs allowed since September 1992, has been the turning point for the Indian stock market. As of now FIIs are allowed to invest in all categories of securities traded in the primary and secondary segments and also in the derivatives segment. The ceiling on aggregate equity of FIIS including NRIs (non-resident Indians) and OCBs (overseas corporate bodies) in a company engaged in activities other than agriculture and plantation has been enhanced in phases from 24 percent to 49 per cent in February 2001.

Following the commissioning of the NSE in June 1994, National Securities Clearing Corporation in April 1996 and National Securities Depository in November 1996, a screen-based, anonymous, order-driven online dematerialized trading has been the order of the day coupled with improved risk management practices for clearing and settlement. Thus, the Indian stock market, which was in isolation until recently, turns out to have been sensitive to developments in the rest of the world by the end of the 1990s. Pursuit of a novel set of policy initiatives with FII portfolio investment and Indian ADR issues at its centre-stage seems to have contributed significantly to the emerging stock market integration. Besides, India's cautious experiment with openness appears to have facilitated the steady pursuit of a policy milieu for stock market integration. In this study, symptomatic analysis will be made on the relation between domestic and foreign equity indices.

2.2 OBJECTIVES OF THE PRESENT STUDY

The following are the objectives of the study;
(1) To explore co-movement in terms of long run relationship among the Indian and American stock markets
(2) To quantify change in co-movement over time series
(3) To study the pattern of risk and return of the selected stock markets

(4) To study the volatility of markets under study and volatility of their correlations

(5) To identify causal relationship of one market with another.

(6) To offer necessary suggestions based on the findings of the study.

2.3   LIMITATIONS OF THE STUDY

(1) The data collected is basically confined to secondary sources, with very little amount of primary data associated with the project.

(2) There is a constraint with regard to time allocated for the research study.

(3) The availability of information in the form of annual reports & price fluctuations of the stock markets is a big constraint to the study.

(4) The data collected for a period of seven months i.e., from January 2012 to July 2012

In this study the statistical tools used are risk, return, average, variance, standard deviation, correlation

2. 4   LITERATURE REVIEW

The nature of the international transmission of stock returns and volatility has been focus of extensive studies. Earlier studies (e.g., Ripley 1973, Lessard 1976, and Hilliard 1979, among many others) generally find low correlations between national stock markets, supporting the benefits of international diversification. The links between national markets have been of heightened interest in the wake of the October 1987 international market crash that saw large, correlated price movements across most stock markets: Eun & Shim (1989), Von Furstenberg and Jeon (1989); King and Wadhwani (1990); Schwert (1990); King et.al. (1994); Longin & Solnik (1995), to name a few.

Table 1: Literature Review

The literature review is summarized in the following table;

Sr. No.	Study	Markets Under Study	Period of Study	Methodology Used	Results Found
1	Eun and Shim (1989)	Australia, Canada, France, Germany, Hong-Kong, Japan, Switzerland, Britain, USA	1980-1985	VAR model, Impulse, Responses	Market Interdependency USA exerts dominant influence
2	Malliaris and Urrutia (1992)	USA, Japan, Britain, Hong Kong, Singapore, Australia	1987-1988	Granger causality test	No Granger causality among markets before and after the crash of October 1987. The dominant role of USA is not confirmed.
3	Bayers and Peel (1993)	USA, Britain, Germany, Japan and Holland	1979-1989	Co-Integration Test	There is no interdependency among the 5 markets and as a result there is no long run relationship among them.

16

4	Richards (1995)	Australia, Austria, Canada, France, Germany, Denmark, Hong Kong, Italy, USA, Japan, Britain,Sweden,Switzerland,Holland, Norway, Spain	1970-1994	Co-integration Test	There is no interdependency among the markets under investigation
5	Choudhry (1997)	Argentina, Brazil, Chile, Colombia, Mexico, Venezuela, USA	1989-1993	Co-integration Test	The markets are co-integrated with or without the presence of the USA which appears to exert domineering influence.
6	Martikainen and Ken (1997)	Denmark, Norway, Sweden, Finland	1988-1994	Multivariate VARFGARCH Model	Independency of markets despite tile trade relations among them. There is an asymmetry in me transmission mechanism of the error variance.
7	Moschos and Xanthakis (1998)	Britain, USA, Greece	1990-1992	Autoregressive Model	The changes of S&P 500 of New-York contribute to improved predictions in the movement of the Athens Stock Exchange. The changes in the Athens Stock Index are attributed mainly on domestic factors.
8	Elyasiasi,Perera and Puri-1998	Sri Lanka,Taiwan, Singapore,Japan,S.Korea, Hong-Kong, India, USA	1989-1994	Multivariate, VAR model	The market of Sri Lanka is not influenced by any other market.
9	Huang, Yang and Hu (2000)	USA, Japan, China, Hong Kong, Taiwan, South China	1992-1997	Co integration test, Granger causality test	There is no co-integration among the countries of the SCGT and also no long –run relationship is found among tile countries of the SCGT and Japan or tile USA. In tile shortrun tile USA market leads tile rest.
10	Gulser Meric, Mitchell Ratner and Ilhan Meric	Israeli, Jordanian, and Turkish, USA and UK	1996-2006	Correlation, Rolling Correlation and Principal Components Analysis	The co-Movements of the Middle East stock markets have not received sufficient attention. The correlation analysis results reveal that there is very low correlation between the Egypt, Israeli, Jordanian, and Turkish stock markets.

These Analysis, Simple Regression, ARCH models etc. and report several empirical features:

(i)   The correlations across the stock markets are time-varying
(ii)   when volatility is high, the price changes in major markets tend to become highly correlated
(iii)   Correlations in volatility and prices appear to be causal from the US market which is the most influential market and none of the other market explains US stock market movements.

The literature concentrated mostly on well-developed equity markets in the U.S., Japan, and Europe, and do not pay much attention to other stock markets. To capture the dynamic inter-linkages between the markets, which have non-overlapping trading hours, the literature largely applied a Two Stage GARCH model with intra-daily data that define overnight and daytime returns.

2.5   DATA

2.5.1. TIME ZONE CONSIDERATIONS

In order to understand the international transmission mechanism between the two markets under consideration, first it is important to recognize that the NSE and NASDAQ markets do not have any overlapping trading hours. There is a time lag of twelve-and-half hours between US Eastern Standard Time and Indian Standard Time. The trading hours of both the markets are shown in below. In Indian Standard Time (IST), NSE opens at 10.00 AM and closes at 3.30 PM.,

Nifty Daily Returns (NIFTYt) = Log (Nifty close on day t / Nifty close on day t-1)*100
NASDAQ Daily Returns (NASDAQt) = Log (NASDAQ close on day t / NASDAQ close on day t-1)*100
S&P 500 Daily Returns (S&P 500t) = = Log (S&P 500 close on day t /S&P 500 close on day t-1)*100
common time interval in which both markets remain open.

Following Hamao et al (1990), Lin et al (1994) and Kee-Hong Bae & Karolyi (1994) to study the synchronization of stock price movements, a daily (close-to-close) return is divided into a day time (open-to-close) and an overnight (close (t-1)-to-open) return for both NSE Nifty and NASDAQ Composite indices. Since there is no overlap between the trading hours of the two markets, it is possible to study the influence of daytime return in one market on the overnight return of the other. Intuitively, traders in India use any relevant information revealed overnight in NASDAQ in pricing their stocks as soon as the opening bell rings. So, the decomposition of daily price changes (returns) into daytime [Close (t)–to-Open (t)] and overnight [Open (t)-to-Close (t-1)] returns is crucial in modeling and understanding how information is transmitted from one market to the other.

2.5.2. DATA SOURCES

In most major stock markets, there are problems in calculating opening prices for these marketindices due to delayed opening of individual stocks. Stoll& Whaley (1990) report that after themarket opens for the first transaction to occur on an average it takes 5 minutes for large stocks and67 minutes for small stocks in NYSE for the first transaction to occur after the market opens. Whendelays occur, the prior day closing prices are used for the unavailable current price in calculating thehigh-frequency index of stock market. This creates artificial serial correlations in close-to-open andopen-to-close returns, which biases intra day return and volatility estimates. In order to minimize theeffects of these stale prices, the literature suggests one to use the index quotes 15 minutes after thefirst open quote, so that the artificial correlation between the intra-day returns are minimized.

For NSE Nifty, the first open quote of the index is available at around 9.55 AM. At thisfirst open quote, since all the 50 constituent scrips of Nifty have not been traded, taking this value asthe open quote would be inappropriate. But usually by the official opening time of 10.00 AM,around 10,000 trades take place on a typical day in NSE. So we take the open quote of Nifty in theanalysis as its value at 10.00 0'clock. The 10.00 0'clock data of NSE Nifty is provided by NationalStock Exchange Research Initiative. Daily official open(9.30AM, EST) and close (4.00PM, EST)quotes of NASDAQ Composite Index have been downloaded from www.nasdaq.comand that of S& P 500 index are downloaded from www.finance.yahoo.com. For S & P 500 index on most of thedays the open quote of most of is exactly same as that of previous day's close quote havingserious stale quote problems. For NASDAQ Composite index the close quote on day t-1is different from open quote on day t, the stale price effect will be minimal as comparedto S&P 500 index. We unable to get the intra-day data of S & P 500, so as to minimizethe stale quote problem. Hence we unable to use S & P 500 index in our further intra daysimilar to that of NASDAQ. Specifically, in this study, we calculate the returns as follows:

Nifty overnight Returns (NIFONt) = $\log\left(\frac{Nifty\ open\ on\ day\ t}{Nifty\ close\ on\ day\ t-1}\right) \times 100$

Nifty Daytime Returns (NIFDt) = $\log\left(\frac{Nifty\ close\ on\ day\ t}{Nifty\ open\ on\ day\ t}\right) \times 100$

NASDAQ Overnight Returns (NASONt)=$\log\left(\frac{NASDAQ\ open\ on\ day\ t}{NASDAQ\ close\ on\ day\ t-1}\right) \times 100$

NASDAQ Daytime Returns (NASDt)=$\log\left(\frac{NASDAQ\ close\ on\ day\ t}{NASDAQ\ open\ on\ day\ t}\right) \times 100$

2.5.3 DATA
PRIMARY DATA:

Data which is collected from first-hand-experience is known as primary data. Primary data has not been published yet and is more reliable, authentic and objective. Primary data is not changed or altered by human beings, therefore its validity is greater than secondary data.

SOURCES OF PRIMARY DATA

Sources for primary data are limited and at times it becomes difficult to obtain data from primary source because of either scarcity of population or lack of cooperation. Regardless of any difficulty one can face in collecting primary data; it is the most authentic and reliable data source. Some of the sources of primary data are Experiments, surveys.

SECONDARY DATA

Data collected from a source that has already been published in any form is called secondary data. The review of literature in any research is based on secondary data. Mostly from books, journals and periodicals.

SOURCES OF SECONDARY DATA

Secondary data is often readily available. Because of electronic media and internet the availability of secondary data has become much easier.

PUBLISHED PRINTED SOURCES

There are variety of published printed sources. Their credibility depends on many factors. For example, on the writer, publishing company and time and date when published. New sources are preferred and old sources should be avoided as new technology and researches bring new facts into light. For example books, journals/periodicals, magazines/newspapers, etc.,

PUBLISHED ELECTRONIC SOURCES

As internet is becoming more advance, fast and reachable to the masses; it has been seen that much information that is not available in printed form is available on internet. In the past the credibility of internet was questionable but today it is not. The reason is that in the past journals and books were seldom published on internet but today almost every journal and book is available online. Some are free and for others you have to pay the price. For example e-journals, general websites, weblogs, etc.,

UNPUBLISHED PERSONAL RECORDs

Some unpublished data may also be useful in some cases. For example diaries, letters

GOVERNEMENT RECORDS

Government records are very important for marketing, management, humanities and social science research. For example Census Data/population statistics, Health records, Educational institutes records

My project work is based on secondary sources of data only

2.6   HYPOTHESES

The present study is directed towards studying the dynamics between stock returns volatility and exchange ratesmovement. We focus our study towards Nifty returns and Indian Rupee-US Dollar Exchange Rates. Thefrequency of data is kept at daily level and time span of study is taken from January 1, 2012 to July31, 2012.The

results from daily data are more precise and are better able to capture the dynamics between exchange ratesand Nifty index. The data consists of – i) daily closing prices of the Nifty index , used to compute stock returnsand ii) Indian Rupee/US Dollar ratios on a daily basis, used to compute exchange rates. The daily returns andexchange rates have been matched by calendar date. Data has been taken from NSE INDIA(http://www.nseindia.com/content/indices/ind_histvalues.htm)and NASDAQ (www.nasdaq.com)..Daily stock returns have been calculated by taking the natural logarithm of the daily closing price relatives,
i.e. r= ln P(t)/P(t-1) ,where P(t) is the closing price of the tth day. Similarly, natural logarithm of the daily exchangerate relatives have been computed as ln E(t)/E(t-1). The values so obtained have been employed for studying therelationship between NSE stock returns and NASDAQ returns. Line plots of the two, so obtained, normalized series areshown in Fig 1.1 and 1.2 respectively.

After reviewing the existing literature,following hypotheses are formulated in order to study the behavior of thetwo variables and were then put on test for the collected data to address the objective of the study:

Hypothesis 1: Stock returns and exchange rates are not normally distributed.
Hypothesis 2: Unit Root exists (i.e. non stationarity) in both the series.
Hypothesis 3: Correlation exists between the two variables-Stock returns and Exchange rates.
Hypothesis 4: No Causality exists between stock returns and exchange rates.
Following methods/tools are used to test the above hypotheses and subsequently draw inferences about thebehavior and dynamics of the two variables. The tests- namely, the JB Test, Unit root test - were conducted with the aid of computer software.

2.7 TOOLS AND TECHNIQUES OF ANALYSIS

ARITHMETIC AVERAGE OR MEAN :

The arithmetic average measures the central tendency . The purpose of computing an average value for a set of observations is to obtain a single value, which is representative of all the items. The main objective of averaging is to arrive at a single value which is a representative of the characteristics of the entire mass of data and arithmetic average or mean of a series(usually denoted by x) is the value obtained by dividing the sum of the values of various items in a series (sigma x) divided by the number of items (N) constituting the series.

Thus, if X1,X2……………..Xn are the given N observations. Then

$$\bar{X} = \frac{X_1 + X_2 + \cdots + X_n}{N}$$

STANDARD DEVIATION

The concept of standard deviation was first suggested by Karl Pearson in 1983.it may be defined as the positive square root of the arithmetic mean of the squares of deviations of the given observations from their arithmetic mean. In short S.D may be defined as "Root Mean Square Deviation from Mean". It is by far the most important and widely used measure of studying dispersions.

For a set of N observations X1,X2........Xn with mean X,
Deviations from Mean: (X1-),(X2-X),....(Xn-X)
Mean-square deviations from Mean:
$$= 1/N \ (X1-X)2+(X2-X)2+..........+(Xn-X)2$$
$$=1/N \ sigma(X-X)2$$

VARIANCE

The square of standard deviation is known as Variance. Variance is the square root of the standard deviation:

Variance $=(S.D)2$

Where,(S.D)is standard deviation

CORRELATION

Correlation is a statistical technique, which measures and analyses the degree or extent to which two or more variables fluctuate with reference to one another. Correlation thus denotes the inter-dependence amongst variables. The degrees are expressed by a coefficient, which ranges between –1 and +1. The direction of change is indicated by (+) or (-) signs. The former refers to a sympathetic movement in a same direction and the later in the opposite direction. Karl Pearson's method of calculating coefficient (r) is based on covariance of the concerned variables. It was devised by Karl Pearson a great British Biometrician. This measure known as Pearsonian correlation coefficient between two variables (series) X and Y usually denoted by 'r' is a numerical measure of linear relationship and is defined as the ratio of the covariance between X and Y (written as Cov(X,Y) to the product of standard deviation of X and Y

Symbolically

$$\rho = \frac{Cov\ (X,Y)}{SD\ of\ X,Y}$$

$$= \frac{\Sigma(x-\bar{x})(y-\bar{y})}{SD\ of\ X,Y}$$

$$= \frac{\Sigma XY}{N}$$

Σxy = sum of the product of deviations in X and Y series calculated with reference to their arithmetic means.

X = standard deviation of the series X.

Y = standard deviation of the series Y.

NORMALITY TEST

The Jarque-Bera (JB) test is used to test whether stock returns and exchange rates individually follow the normal probability distribution. The JB test of normality is an asymptotic, or large-sample, test. This test computes the skewness and kurtosis measures and uses the following test statistic:

$JB = n [S^2/6 + (K-3)^2/24]$

Where n = sample size, S = skewness coefficient, and K = kurtosis coefficient. For a normally distributed variable, S = 0 and K = 3. Therefore, the JB test of normality is a test of the joint hypothesis that S and K are 0 and 3 respectively.

UNIT ROOT TEST (STATIONARITY TEST)

Empirical work based on time series data assumes that the underlying time series is stationary. Broadly speaking a data series is said to be stationary if its mean and variance are constant (non-changing) over time and the value of covariance between two time periods depends only on the distance or lag between the two time periods and not on the actual time at which the covariance is computed [Gujrati (2003)].A unit root test has been applied to check whether a series is stationary or not. Stationarity condition has been tested using Augmented Dickey Fuller(ADF) [Dickey and Fuller (1979, 1981), Gujarati (2003), Enders (1995)].

AUGMENTED DICKEY–FULLER (ADF) TEST

Augmented Dickey-Fuller (ADF) test has been carried out which is the modified version of Dickey-Fuller (DF) test. ADF makes a parametric correction in the original DF test for higher-order correlation by assuming that the series follows an AR (p) process. The ADF approach controls for higher-order correlation by adding lagged difference terms of the dependent variable to the right-hand side of the regression.

The Augmented Dickey-Fuller test specification used here is as follows:

$$\_Y_t = b_0 + \_Y_{t-1} + \mu_1 \_Y_{t-1} + \mu_2 \_Y_{t-2} + \ldots + \mu_p \_Y_{t-p} + e_t$$

Y_t represents time series to be tested, b_0 is the intercept term, _ is the coefficient of interest in the unit root test, μ_i is the parameter of the augmented lagged first difference of Y_t to represent the pth-order autoregressive process, and e_t is the white noise error term.

CHAPTER – III

INDUSTRY AND COMPANY PROFILES

3.1   INDIAN STOCK MARKET

The Indian Equity market is divided in to two parts Primary market - where the share is first issued in the form of IPO (Initial Public Offering) and after issuing the share it is listed on exchange and share is traded on exchange where shares can be bought and sold this is secondary market. In India mainly there are two exchanges – NSE (National Stock Exchange) BSE-Bombay Stock Exchange. The BSE is the oldest exchange in India (started in 1875).NSE started operation on 1994. Before 2000 shares was held in Physical form but the main difficulty with Physical shares is method of transaction which is open outcry system and process is not transparent to investor also Physical shares were prone to duplication and fraud. So in 2000 NSE introduced the electronic screen based trading system further the introduction of Dematerialization (Conversion of physical share in to electronic form) and depository(where the electronic form of share is kept) revolutionized the Indian Stock market. Currently there are mainly two Depository (DP) -NSDL and CDSL and these DP are like bank of share. Individual/Firm can deal through Broker (who is registered and having membership in Exchanges and Depository) for buying and selling securities. Today NSE outpaced BSE in volume of trade. Then what is the purpose of stock market? Stock market serves the company by providing company the finance for long term needs and for investor an opportunity to park their savings in corporate world and in turn give their hand in Nation's development so stock exchange have a very vital role in country's economic development.

To buy the shares investor has to open a trading and demat account. So investor has to approach a broker/sub broker who has member ship in Exchange(where the share is listed mainly NSE and BSE) and depository(where share is kept in Demat form-Electronic form [mainly CDSL and NSDL).Then Investor has to give necessary identity proof, Address proof, Bank proof and fill the KYC form after reading it carefully. broker will ask for power of attorney for smooth transaction but this is not mandatory and if POA is not given investor had to fill the delivery instruction slip after selling the share. After opening the account the investor can do trading/investing Directly, Through Phone Internet form broking office and he will contract note(similar to bill that we got when we purchase something and contract note include all minute detail of transaction including brokerage [commission of broking house] STT and Other taxes) for the transaction done by him within 24 hr of transaction and he has to give cheque to Broker in the name of broking office (no cash transaction is permitted) and current settlement is rolling settlement (The rolling settlement ensures that each day's trade is settled by keeping a fixed gap of a specified number of working days between a trade and its settlement. At present, this gap is 3 working days after the trading day. So transaction entered into on Day 1 has to be settled on the Day 1 + 3 working days, when funds pay in or securities pay out takes place. If investor is selling the security he will get money in 3 working days. If investor failed to deliver the security within time his share will get auctioned and investor has to borne the penalty. If the investor has old physical share he can fill the dematerialization form and send it for converting it to demat form. The reverse can also be done. General purpose of Stock Market is for Investment but bulk of activities done in market is day trading. Day trading means BUYING/SELLING of shares and offsetting the position on same day. Day traders serves the purpose of bringing the liquidity to market and they help the market movement and more than 80% of the volume from market is coming from day trading. Introduction of derivative market had made the day trading to grow more and introduction of advanced day trading technique. The main tool for Stock market investment/trading are Fundamental analysis -which studies about the fundamental of companies and economy and Technical Analysis-which studies the market by analyzing the past movement of share and market. The investment scenario in India is now is at par with global Market. The introduction of Derivative, Currency, Commodity market now helped the Indian Investor to Invest in almost anything like Share, Commodity, Currency, Bonds and complex thing like Interest rate future, Weather Derivative, Volatility Index and more and Stock market are giving various product to invest in with various amount of risk like bonds, Gold ETF, Equity and Preference Share, Commodities (metal and Agriculture) Currency to high risk Derivative product.

3.2   AMERICAN STOCK MARKET

3.2.1 HISTORY OF AMERICAN STOCK MARKET

In the 1700s groups of brokers in Philadelphia, Pennsylvania, and New York City began to meet in parks and coffeehouses to buy and sell securities. In open auctions, traders called out names of companies and numbers of shares available. Shares went to the highest bidders. In 1800 the Philadelphia Board of Brokers drew up regulations and a constitution and set up central offices where trading could take place. The organization they created, the Philadelphia Stock Exchange, is the oldest exchange in the United States. In 1817 brokers in New York formed the New York Stock and Exchange Board (renamed the New York Stock Exchange in 1863). As the United States grew and prospered during the 19th century, many more companies began to issue stocks and bonds. More people began to invest, and dozens of exchanges were formed across the country. Some of these are still in existence, but many others were short-lived. For example, the California gold rush of 1849 gave birth to a number of small exchanges where the public could buy shares in the new mining companies. As the gold rush subsided, these companies went out of business and the exchanges closed. During the 1920s millions of Americans began to purchase stocks for the first time. Stock prices rose steadily as inflated market demand outpaced increases in the value of the real assets of these businesses as well as their profits. Investors eventually realized that a large imbalance existed between stock prices and the real assets available to back them up, including profits, and decided to sell. On October 29, 1929, great numbers of people tried to sell their stocks all at once. Prices tumbled so drastically on the NYSE and other exchanges that the event became known as the crash of 1929. Millions of investors lost their savings in the crash, and many found themselves deeply in debt because they could not repay the money they had borrowed to buy stocks. During the years immediately following the crash, most investors refused to put any more money in stocks. The lack of investment funds contributed to the Great Depression of the 1930s, an economic crisis that left one of every four American workers unemployed and resulted in widespread poverty. In the 1980s and 1990s stock exchanges achieved new levels of market efficiency through their increased use of fast and inexpensive computers. Computer networks allowed exchanges to connect to each other, both within countries and internationally. Electronic exchanges fostered the growth of an open, global securities market. In 1987 the stock market experienced a brief, but major crash, marked by a more than 20 percent decline; over one day's trading, in the Standard & Poor's index of stock prices. Markets in other countries have experienced periods of severe decline as well.

Economists linked the 1987 U.S. crash to the use by traders of new markets for low-margin stock index futures. The period from 1990 to early 2000 saw a significant rise in stock prices. The growth resulted in the longest period of average increases in stock prices in the history of the United States. The market value of the outstanding shares of domestically issued stock rose from about $3.5 trillion to approximately $20 trillion. But then stock prices began to decline. By the middle of 2002 the market value of the outstanding shares of domestically issued stock stood at about $13.3 trillion. The earlier period of rising stock prices, from 1990 to the first part of 2000, was known as a bull market. The bull market was linked to the strong national economy. A continued expansion of production and employment made investors optimistic about business profits and increased the demand for securities. This growth in demand was especially true for technology companies. In the latter half of the bull market the dot.com phenomenon developed. Small startup companies specializing in sales on the Internet began to issue stock. The prices of these stocks rose rapidly with strong demand, based on the belief that this new way of doing business would generate enormous profits.

The end of the bull market in 2000 and the beginning of a bear market (period of declining stock prices) was marked by several factors. One was the end of the national economic expansion with a decline in production and a rise in unemployment. Another was the end of the dot.com phenomenon when investors recognized that it was going to be much more difficult than originally forecast for these companies to become profitable. In 2001 the September 11 attacks by terrorists on the World Trade Center and the Pentagon also had predictable negative consequences for securities markets.

3.2.2 DOW, S&P500, NY AND NASDAQ COMPARISON

At a first glance the NYSE and NASDAQ markets may be very hard to find a difference between them because they seem very similar. The NYSE is defined as an actual physical place unlike NASDAQ. NYSE uses an auction market floor located in New York City on Wall Street, which uses floor traders to make most of their transactions. Every stock that is listed in the NYSE has a special holder which facilitates and oversees every trade made for that particular stock. In order to buy a stock on the NYSE you have to tell your broker which will then call the broker on the floor, or enter it into the DOT system. Like I said with NASDAQ though, there is no physical placed that it exists unlike the NYSE. NASDAQ uses an over the counter market method and relies on broker dealer firms in order to maintain and trade its stocks. NASDAQ is not an auction market like the NYSE but rather a communications network between thousands of computers. Broker dealer firms, or market makers, places there names on a list of buyers and sellers and then NASDAQ proceeds to distribute this information in a split second to thousands of computers. At anytime if you wish to buy or sell your stocks on NASDAQ all you have to do is call your market maker, example would be Microsoft which has several, and they will enter the information of your trade or you can enter your order in a NASDAQ online execution system. In conclusion, NYSE is a physical place where you trade stocks on a market floor with floor brokers, NADAQ on the other hand is an online communications system that uses brokers and market makers in order to sell and trade stocks.

The Dow Jones Industrial Average is traditionally the most watched index however the most technical analysts use the S&P 500 to examine the US economy. The major difference between the Dow and the S&P 500 indexes is how they're calculated. The Dow is price-weighted while the S&P 500 is value-weighted. The S&P 500 index is calculated by taking the number of shares in circulation of each company and multiplying them by the share value and the sum is the index. In the Dow average only one share from each company is used and the sum is divided by the number of companies. The problem with the Dow index is stocks with higher share prices are given far more weight than cheaper stocks. An example of this problem, General Electric and Microsoft, some of the most valued companies in the index, have a small weighted value (GE stands around $35 and MSFT at $29, against Johnson & Johnson at $65). Another problem with a price-weighted index is that each dollar change of a component affects the average by the same amount. One can have a situation where an equivalent percentage change in the most expensive stock, say IBM, can be worth around five times the lowest priced constituent, such as Intel.

3.3   NATIONAL STOCK EXCHANGE

The **National   Stock   Exchange** (NSE)   is stock   exchange located at Mumbai, Maharashtra, India. It is in the top 20 largest stock exchanges in the world by market capitalization and largest in India by daily turnover and number of trades, for both equities and derivative trading. NSE has a market capitalization of around US$1 trillion and over 1,652 listings as of July 2012. Though a number of other exchanges exist, NSE and the Bombay Stock Exchange are the two most significant stock exchanges in India, and between them are responsible for the vast majority of share transactions. The NSE's key index is the S&P CNX Nifty, known as the NSE **NIFTY** (National Stock Exchange Fifty), an index of fifty major stocks weighted by market capitalization.

NSE is mutually owned by a set of leading financial institutions, banks, insurance companies and other financial intermediaries in India but its ownership and management operate as separate entities. There are at least 2 foreign investors NYSE Euronext and Goldman Sachs who have taken a stake in the NSE. As of 2006, the NSE VSAT terminals, 2799 in total, cover more than 1500 cities across India. In 2011, NSE was the third largest stock exchange in the world in terms of the number of contracts (1221 million) traded in equity derivatives. It is the second fastest growing stock exchange in the world with a recorded growth of 16.6%.

3.3.1 ORIGINS

The National Stock Exchange of India was set up by Government of India on the recommendation of Pherwani Committee in 1991.Promoted by leading Financial institutions essentially led by IDBI at the behest of the Government of India, it was incorporated in November 1992 as a tax-paying company. In April 1993, it was recognized as a stock exchange under the Securities Contracts (Regulation) Act, 1956. NSE commenced operations in the Wholesale Debt Market (WDM) segment in June 1994. The Capital market (Equities) segment of the NSE commenced operations in November 1994, while operations in the Derivatives segment commenced in June 2000.

3.3.2 MARKETS

Currently, NSE has the following major segments of the capital market:

Equities

- Equities
- Indices
- Mutual Funds
- Exchange Traded Funds
- Initial Public Offerings
- Security Lending and Borrowing Scheme

Derivatives

- Equity Derivatives (including Global Indices like S&P 500, Dow Jones and FTSE)
- Currency Derivatives
- Interest Rate Futures

Debt

- Retail Debt Market
- Wholesale Debt Market
- Corporate Bonds

Equity Derivatives The National Stock Exchange of India Limited (NSE) commenced trading in derivatives with the launch of index futures on June 12, 2000. The futures and options segment of NSE has made a mark for itself globally. In the Futures and Options segment, trading in S&P CNX Nifty Index, CNX IT index, Bank Nifty Index, Nifty Midcap 50 index and single stocks are available. Trading in Mini Nifty Futures & Options and Long term Options on S&P CNX Nifty are also available. The average daily turnover in the F&O Segment of the Exchange during 2009-10 was ` 72,392 crore (US $ 16,097 million)

On August 29, 2011, National Stock exchange launced derivative contracts on the world's most followed equity indices, the S&P 500 and the Dow Jones Industrial Average. This was the first time that derivative contracts on global indices are available in India. This is the also the first time in the world that futures contracts on the S&P 500 index were introduced and listed on an exchange outside of their home country, USA. The new contracts include futures on both the DJIA and the S&P 500, and options on the S&P 500. The first day volumes at the close of trading on August 29, 2011 at 3.30 pm, on the 2 indices in futures and options contracts was nearly Rs 122 crores (1220 million).

On May 3, 2012,The National Stock exchange launched derivative contracts (futures and options) on FTSE 100, the widely tracked index of the UK equity stock market. This was the first of its kind for an index of the UK equity stock market to be launched in India. FTSE 100 includes 100 largest UK listed blue chip companies and has given returns of 17.8 per cent on investment over three years. The index constitutes 85.6 per cent of UK's equity market cap. NSE recorded a volume of 500 crores (5000 million) on the 1st day of trading

Currency Derivatives : In August 2008 currency derivatives were introduced in India with the launch of Currency Futures in USD INR by NSE. It also added currency futures in euros, pounds and yen. Interest Rate Futures were introduced for the first time in India by NSE on 31 August 2009, exactly one year after the launch of Currency Futures.

Debt Market : NSE became the first stock exchange to get approval for interest rate futures, As recommended by SEBI-RBI committee, on 31 August 2009, a futures contract based on 7% 10 Year Government of India (Notional) was launched with quarterly maturities.

3.3.3 TRADING SCHEDULE

Trading takes place on all days of the week except Saturdays & Sundays. The market timings are as follows:

(1) Pre-open session (Regular)

- Order entry & modification Open: **09:00 hrs**
- Order entry & modification Close: **09:08 hrs**[*]

[*]with random closure in last one minute. Pre-open order matching starts immediately after close of pre-open order entry.

(2) Pre-open Session for IPO and Relist Securities

- Order entry & modification Open: **09:00 hrs**
- Order entry & modification Close: **09:45 hrs**[*]

[*] with random closure in last one minute. Pre-open order matching starts immediately after close of pre-open order entry.

(3) Regular trading session

- Normal Market Open: **09:15 hrs**
- Normal Market Close: **15:30 hrs**

Block deal session is held between **09:15 hrs** and **09:50 hrs**.

(4) The Closing Session is held between **15.40 hrs** and **16.00 hrs**.

The Exchange may also extend, advance or reduce trading hours when its deems fit and necessary.

3.3.4 EXCHANGE TRADED FUNDS ON NSE

ETF's launched on NSE Exchange Traded Funds are essentially Index Funds that are listed and traded on exchanges like stocks. An ETF is a basket of stocks that reflects the composition of an Index, like S&P CNX Nifty. The ETFs trading value is based on the net asset value of the underlying stocks that it represents.

ETF's Scheme launched on NSE

- Equity
- Gold
- Debt
- World Indices

In recent times, Exchange-traded funds (ETFs) have gained a wider acceptance as financial instruments whose unique advantages over mutual funds have caught the eye of many an investor. These instruments are beneficial for Investors that find it difficult to master the tricks of the trade of analyzing and picking stocks for their portfolio. Various mutual funds provide ETF products that attempt to replicate the indices on NSE, so as to provide returns that closely correspond to the total returns of the securities represented in the index.

3.3.5 CERTIFICATIONS

NSE also conducts online examination and awards certification, under its programmes of NSE's Certification in Financial Markets (NCFM)[1]. Currently, certifications are available in 32 modules, covering different sectors of financial and capital markets, both at beginner and advanced levels. the list of the various modules can be found at the following official site of NSE India.[2] Branches of the NSE are located throughout India. NSE, in collaboration with reputed colleges and institutes in India, has been offering a short-term course called NSE Certified Capital Market Professional (NCCMP) since August 2009, in the campuses of the respective colleges/ institutes.

3.4 NASDAQ

The NASDAQ, an acronym for National Association of Securities Dealers Automated Quotations, is an electronic stock exchange with 3,300 company listings. It currently has a greater trading volume than any other U.S. exchange, making approximately 1.8 billion trades per day. The NYSE is still considered the biggest exchange because its market capitalization far exceeds that of the NASDAQ. The NASDAQ trades shares in a variety of companies, but is well known for being a high-tech exchange, trading many new, high growth, and volatile stocks. This is partially due to the fact that the listing fees on the NASDAQ are significantly lower than those for the NYSE, with the maximum price only $150,000. The NASDAQ is a publicly owned company, trading its shares on its own exchange under the ticker symbol NDAQ.

3.4.1 HISTORY

NASDAQ was founded in 1971 by the National Association of Securities Dealers (NASD), who divested themselves of it in a series of sales in 2000 and 2001. It is owned and operated by the NASDAQ OMX Group, the stock of which was listed on its own stock exchange beginning July 2, 2002, under the ticker symbol **NASDAQ**: NDAQ. It is regulated by the Financial Industry Regulatory Authority (FINRA), the successor to the NASD.

When the NASDAQ stock exchange began trading on February 8, 1971, it was the world's first electronic stock market. At first, it was merely a computer bulletin board system and did not actually connect buyers and sellers. The NASDAQ helped lower the spread (the difference between the bid price and the ask price of the stock) but somewhat paradoxically was unpopular among brokerages because they made much of their money on the spread.

NASDAQ was the successor to the over-the-counter (OTC) system of trading. As late as 1987, the NASDAQ exchange was still commonly referred to as the OTC in media and also in the monthly Stock Guides issued by Standard & Poor's Corporation.

Over the years, NASDAQ became more of a stock market by adding trade and volume reporting and automated trading systems. NASDAQ was also the first stock market in the United States to start trading online. Nobody before them had ever done this, highlighting NASDAQ-traded companies (usually in technology) and closing with the declaration that NASDAQ is "the stock market for the next hundred years." Its main index is the NASDAQ Composite, which has been published since its inception. However, its exchange-traded fund tracks the large-cap NASDAQ-

100index, which was introduced in 1985 alongside the NASDAQ 100 Financial Index.

Until 1987, most trading occurred via the telephone, but during the October 1987 stock market crash, market makers often didn't answer their phones. To counteract this, the Small Order Execution System (SOES) was established, which provides an electronic method for dealers to enter their trades. NASDAQ requires market makers to honor trades over SOES.

In 1992, it joined with the London Stock Exchange to form the first intercontinental linkage of securities markets. NASD spun off NASDAQ in 2000 to form a publicly traded company, the NASDAQ Stock Market, Inc.

In 2006 NASDAQ changed from stock market to licensed national exchange.

On November 8, 2007, NASDAQ bought the Philadelphia Stock Exchange (PHLX) for US$652 million. PHLX is the oldest stock exchange in America—having been in operation since 1790.

To qualify for listing on the exchange, a company must be registered with the United States Securities and Exchange Commission (SEC), have at least three market makers (financial firms that act as brokers or dealers for specific securities) and meet minimum requirements for assets, capital, public shares, and shareholders.

In February, 2011, in the wake of an announced merger of NYSE Euronext with Deutsche Börse, speculation developed that Nasdaq and Intercontinental Exchange (ICE) could mount a counter-bid of their own for NYSE. Nasdaq could be looking to acquire the American exchange's cash equities business, ICE the derivatives business. As of the time of the speculation, "NYSE Euronext's market value was $9.75 billion. Nasdaq was valued at $5.78 billion, while ICE was valued at $9.45 billion." Late in the month, Nasdaq was reported to be considering asking either ICE or the Chicago Merc to join in what would probably have to be, if it proceeded, an $11–12 billion counterbid.

EASDAQ (European Association of Securities Dealers Automatic Quotation System) founded originally as a European equivalent to NASDAQ, it was purchased by NASDAQ in 2001 and became NASDAQ Eur03, it shut down operations as a result of the burst of the dot-com bubble. In 2007, NASDAQ Europe was revived as Equiduct and is currently operating under Börse Berlin.

3.4.2 QUOTE AVAILABILITY

NASDAQ quotes are available at three levels

- Level 1 shows the highest bid and lowest offer—the inside quote.
- Level 2 shows all public quotes of market makers together with information of market dealers wishing to sell or buy stock and recently executed orders.
- Level 3 is used by the market makers and allows them to enter their quotes and execute orders.

3.4.3 TRADING SCHEDULE

NASDAQ has a pre-market session from 7:00am to 9:30am, a normal trading session from 9:30am to 4:00pm and a post-market session from 4:00pm to 8:00pm (all times in ET).

3.4.4 INDICES

- NASDAQ-100
- NASDAQ Bank
- NASDAQ Biotechnology Index
- NASDAQ Transportation Index
- NASDAQ Composite

3.4.5 MARKET TIERS

- NASDAQ Capital Market – Small Cap
- NASDAQ Global Market – Mid cap
- NASDAQ Global Select Market – Large Cap

CHAPTER – IV

RESULTS AND DISCUSSION

4.1   RETURN, VARIANCE AND STANDARD DEVIATION OF NSE FOR THE MONTH OF JANUARY – 2012

Sr. No	date	close	returns (x)	$(x - \overline{\overline{x}})$	$(x - \overline{x})^2$
1	02-Jan-12	4636.75	-0.0743	-0.6023	0.3628
2	03-Jan-12	4765.3	2.7724	2.2445	5.0377
3	04-Jan-12	4749.65	-0.3284	-0.8564	0.7334
4	05-Jan-12	4749.95	0.0063	-0.5216	0.2721
5	06-Jan-12	4754.1	0.0874	-0.4406	0.1941
6	07-Jan-12	4746.9	-0.1514	-0.6794	0.4616
7	09-Jan-12	4742.8	-0.0864	-0.6143	0.3774
8	10-Jan-12	4849.55	2.2508	1.7228	2.9682
9	11-Jan-12	4860.95	0.2351	-0.2929	0.0858
10	12-Jan-12	4831.25	-0.6110	-1.1389	1.2972
11	13-Jan-12	4866	0.7193	0.1913	0.0366
12	16-Jan-12	4873.9	0.1624	-0.3656	0.1337
13	17-Jan-12	4967.3	1.9163	1.3884	1.9276
14	18-Jan-12	4955.8	-0.2315	-0.7595	0.5768
15	19-Jan-12	5018.4	1.2632	0.7352	0.5406
16	20-Jan-12	5048.6	0.6018	0.0738	0.0055
17	23-Jan-12	5046.25	-0.0465	-0.5745	0.3300
18	24-Jan-12	5127.35	1.6071	1.0792	1.1647
19	25-Jan-12	5158.3	0.6036	0.0757	0.0057
20	27-Jan-12	5204.7	0.8995	0.3716	0.1381
21	30-Jan-12	5087.3	-2.2556	-2.7836	7.7484
22	31-Jan-12	5199.25	2.2006	1.6726	2.7977
n = 22			$\sum x$ = 11.6148		$\sum (x - \overline{x})^2$ = 27.1953

DESCRIPTIVE STATISTICS	
Mean $\left(\frac{\sum x}{n}\right)$	0.527944498
Median $\left(\frac{n+1}{2}\right)$	0.198712182
Standard Deviation $\left(\sqrt{variance}\right)$	1.111822986
Sample Variance $\left(\frac{\sum(x-\bar{x})2}{n}\right)$	1.236150352
Range	5.028069568
Minimum	-2.255653544
Maximum	2.772416024

4.1.1 JARQUE-BERA TEST :

JB (Observed value)	0.080
JB (Critical value)	5.991
DF	2
p-value	0.961
alpha	0.05

TEST INTERPRETATION:

H0: The variable from which the sample was extracted follows a Normal distribution.
Ha: The variable from which the sample was extracted does not follow a Normal distribution.
As the computed p-value is greater than the significance level alpha=0.05, one cannot reject the null hypothesis H0.
The risk to reject the null hypothesis H0 while it is true is 96.09%.

CRITICAL VALUE:

value of the statistic under the null hypothesis for the probability 1-alpha (right-tailed test)
reject the null hypothesis when the observed value is greater than the critical value

ONE - TAILED p-VALUE:

probability under the null hypothesis to obtain a result as extreme as the observed result, towards the right-tail of the distribution.
reject the null hypothesis when the probability is lower than the alpha level.

4.1.2 CONCLUSION:

At the level of significance Alpha=0.050 the decision is to not reject the null hypothesis that the sample follows a normal distribution.
In other words, the non-normality is not significant.

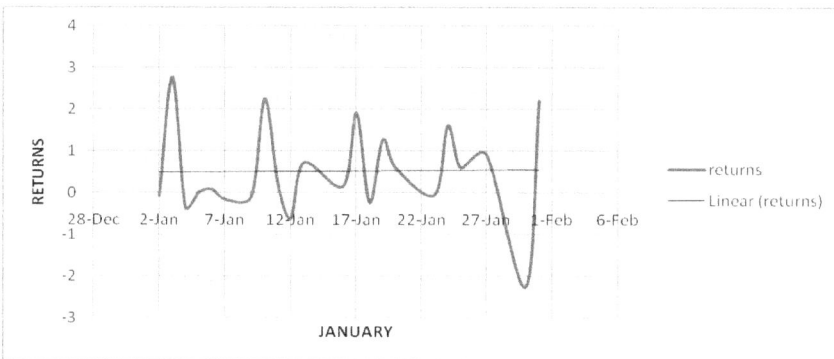

4.1.3 AUGMENTED DICKEY FULLER TEST RESULTS ON NSE RETURNS FOR THE MONTH OF JANUARY 2012

Null Hypothesis: NSE RETURNS for the month of JANUARY has a unit root
Exogenous: Constant
Lag Length: 1 (Fixed)

		t-Statistic	Prob.*
Augmented Dickey-Fuller test statistic		-4.451760	0.0025
Test critical values:	1% level	-3.808546	
	5% level	-3.020686	
	10% level	-2.650413	

*MacKinnon (1996) one-sided p-values.

Augmented Dickey-Fuller Test Equation
Dependent Variable: D(JANUARY RETURNS)
Method: Least Squares

Sample (adjusted): 04/01/2012 - 31/01/2012
Included observations: 20 after adjustments

Variable	Coefficient	Std. Error	t-Statistic	Prob.
RETURNS(-1)	-1.726435	0.387810	-4.451760	0.0004
D(RETURNS(-1))	0.224761	0.257074	0.874307	0.3941
C	0.808591	0.301617	2.680854	0.0158

R-squared	0.754171	Mean dependent var	-0.028590
Adjusted R-squared	0.725250	S.D. dependent var	1.871140
S.E. of regression	0.980789	Akaike info criterion	2.936562
Sum squared resid	16.35309	Schwarz criterion	3.085922
Log likelihood	-26.36562	Hannan-Quinn criter.	2.965718
F-statistic	26.07684	Durbin-Watson stat	2.171884
Prob(F-statistic)	0.000007		

The t-Statistic (-4.451760) is lower than the Critical Values at 1%, 5% and 10% significant levels (-3.808546, -3.020686 and -2.650413 respectively). Hence the null hypothesis is rejected and it is concluded that the returns for the month of January 2012 are stationary.

4.2 RETURN, VARIANCE AND STANDARD DEVIATION OF NSE FOR THE MONTH OF FEBRUARY – 2012

s.no	date	close	returns (x)	$(x - \overline{x})$	$(x - \overline{x})^2$
1	01-Feb-12	5235.7	0.72	0.54	0.29
2	02-Feb-12	5269.9	0.65	0.47	0.22
3	03-Feb-12	5325.85	1.06	0.88	0.77
4	06-Feb-12	5361.65	0.67	0.49	0.24
5	07-Feb-12	5335.15	-0.49	-0.68	0.46
6	08-Feb-12	5368.15	0.62	0.44	0.19
7	09-Feb-12	5412.35	0.82	0.64	0.41
8	10-Feb-12	5381.6	-0.57	-0.75	0.56
9	13-Feb-12	5390.2	0.16	-0.02	0.00
10	14-Feb-12	5416.05	0.48	0.30	0.09
11	15-Feb-12	5531.95	2.14	1.96	3.83
12	16-Feb-12	5521.95	-0.18	-0.36	0.13
13	17-Feb-12	5564.3	0.77	0.58	0.34
14	21-Feb-12	5607.15	0.77	0.59	0.34
15	22-Feb-12	5505.35	-1.82	-2.00	3.99
16	23-Feb-12	5483.3	-0.40	-0.58	0.34
17	24-Feb-12	5429.3	-0.98	-1.17	1.36
18	27-Feb-12	5281.2	-2.73	-2.91	8.47
19	28-Feb-12	5375.5	1.79	1.60	2.57
20	29-Feb-12	5385.2	0.18	0.00	0.00
n = 20			$\sum x = 3.66$		$\sum (x - \bar{x})^2 = 24.62$

DESCRIPTIVE STATISTICS	
Mean $\left(\frac{\sum x}{n}\right)$	0.183096147
Median $\left(\frac{n+1}{2}\right)$	0.549056676
Standard Deviation $\left(\sqrt{variance}\right)$	1.109539718
Sample Variance $\left(\frac{\sum(x-\bar{x})2}{n}\right)$	1.231078386
Range	4.867727728
Minimum	-2.727791796
Maximum	2.139935931

4.2.1 JARQUE-BERA TEST :

JB (Observed value)	2.552
JB (Critical value)	5.991
DF	2
p-value	0.279
alpha	0.05

TEST INTERPRETATION:

H0: The variable from which the sample was extracted follows a Normal distribution.
Ha: The variable from which the sample was extracted does not follow a Normal distribution.
As the computed p-value is greater than the significance level alpha=0.05, one cannot reject the null hypothesis H0.
The risk to reject the null hypothesis H0 while it is true is 27.91%.

CRITICAL VALUE:
value of the statistic under the null hypothesis for the probability 1-alpha (right-tailed test)
reject the null hypothesis when the observed value is greater than the critical value

ONE - TAILED p-VALUE:
probability under the null hypothesis to obtain a result as extreme as the observed result, towards the right-tail of the distribution.
reject the null hypothesis when the probability is lower than the alpha level.

4.2.2 CONCLUSION:
At the level of significance Alpha=0.050 the decision is to not reject the null hypothesis that the sample follows a normal distribution.
In other words, the non-normality is not significant.

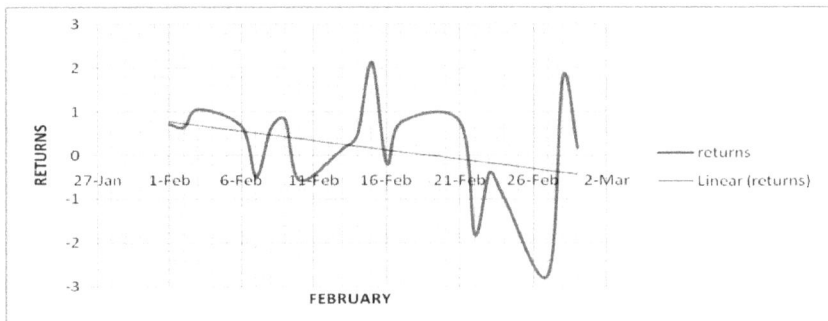

4.2.3 AUGMENTED DICKEY FULLER TEST RESULTS ON NSE RETURNS FOR THE MONTH OF FEBRUARY 2012

Null Hypothesis: NSE RETURNS for the month of FEBRUARY has a unit root
Exogenous: Constant
Lag Length: 1 (Fixed)

		t-Statistic	Prob.*
Augmented Dickey-Fuller test statistic		-2.647206	0.1024
Test critical values:	1% level	-3.857386	
	5% level	-3.040391	
	10% level	-2.660551	

*MacKinnon (1996) one-sided p-values.
NOTE: Probabilities and critical values calculated for 20 observations
  and may not be accurate for a sample size of 18

Augmented Dickey-Fuller Test Equation
Dependent Variable: D(FEBRUARY RETURNS)
Method: Least Squares

Sample (adjusted): 03/02/2012 - 28/02/2012
Included observations: 18 after adjustments

Variable	Coefficient	Std. Error	t-Statistic	Prob.
RETURNS01(-1)	-0.995450	0.376038	-2.647206	0.0183
D(RETURNS01(-1))	-0.030018	0.270476	-0.110980	0.9131
C	0.128309	0.302118	0.424698	0.6771

R-squared	0.516041	Mean dependent var	-0.026111
Adjusted R-squared	0.451513	S.D. dependent var	1.709479
S.E. of regression	1.266039	Akaike info criterion	3.460675
Sum squared resid	24.04283	Schwarz criterion	3.609071
Log likelihood	-28.14608	Hannan-Quinn criter.	3.481137
F-statistic	7.997168	Durbin-Watson stat	2.018505
Prob(F-statistic)	0.004326		

The t-Statistic (-2.647206) is greater than the Critical Values at 1%, 5% and 10% significant levels (-3.857386, -3.040391and -2.660551 respectively). Hence it is failed to reject the null hypothesis and it is concluded that the returns for the month of February 2012 are non-stationary.

4.3 RETURN, VARIANCE AND STANDARD DEVIATION OF NSE FOR THE MONTH OF MARCH – 2012

s.no	date	close	returns (x)	$(x - \overline{\overline{x}})$	$(x - \overline{x})^2$
1	01-Mar-12	5339.75	-0.49	-0.44	0.19
2	02-Mar-12	5359.35	0.37	0.42	0.18
3	03-Mar-12	5359.4	0.00	0.05	0.00
4	05-Mar-12	5280.35	-1.47	-1.42	2.03
5	06-Mar-12	5222.4	-1.10	-1.05	1.09
6	07-Mar-12	5220.45	-0.04	0.01	0.00
7	09-Mar-12	5333.55	2.17	2.22	4.92
8	12-Mar-12	5359.55	0.49	0.54	0.29
9	13-Mar-12	5429.5	1.31	1.36	1.84
10	14-Mar-12	5463.9	0.63	0.69	0.47
11	15-Mar-12	5380.5	-1.53	-1.47	2.17
12	16-Mar-12	5317.9	-1.16	-1.11	1.24
13	19-Mar-12	5257.05	-1.14	-1.09	1.19
14	20-Mar-12	5274.85	0.34	0.39	0.15
15	21-Mar-12	5364.95	1.71	1.76	3.10
16	22-Mar-12	5228.45	-2.54	-2.49	6.21
17	23-Mar-12	5278.2	0.95	1.00	1.01
18	26-Mar-12	5184.25	-1.78	-1.73	2.99
19	27-Mar-12	5243.15	1.14	1.19	1.41
20	28-Mar-12	5194.75	-0.92	-0.87	0.76
21	29-Mar-12	5178.85	-0.31	-0.25	0.06
22	30-Mar-12	5295.55	2.25	2.31	5.31
n = 22			$\sum x = -1.14$		$\sum(x - \bar{x})^2 = 36.62$

DESCRIPTIVE STATISTICS	
Mean $\left(\frac{\sum x}{n}\right)$	-0.051730962
Median $\left(\frac{n+1}{2}\right)$	-0.018203103
Standard Deviation $\left(\sqrt{variance}\right)$	1.290158661
Sample Variance $\left(\frac{\sum(x-\bar{x})2}{n}\right)$	1.664509371
Range	4.797688143
Minimum	-2.544292118
Maximum	2.253396024

4.3.1 JARQUE-BERA TEST :

JB (Observed value)	0.707
JB (Critical value)	5.991
DF	2
p-value	0.702
alpha	0.05

TEST INTERPRETATION:

H0: The variable from which the sample was extracted follows a Normal distribution.
Ha: The variable from which the sample was extracted does not follow a Normal distribution.
As the computed p-value is greater than the significance level alpha=0.05, one cannot
reject the null hypothesis H0.
The risk to reject the null hypothesis H0 while it is true is 70.21%.

CRITICAL VALUE:
value of the statistic under the null hypothesis for the probability 1-alpha (right-tailed test)
reject the null hypothesis when the observed value is greater than the critical value

One - tailed p-value:
probability under the null hypothesis to obtain a result as extreme as the observed
result, towards the right-tail of the distribution.
reject the null hypothesis when the probability is lower than the alpha level.

4.3.2 CONCLUSION:
At the level of significance Alpha=0.050 the decision is to not reject the null hypothesis
that the sample follows a normal distribution.
In other words, the non-normality is not significant.

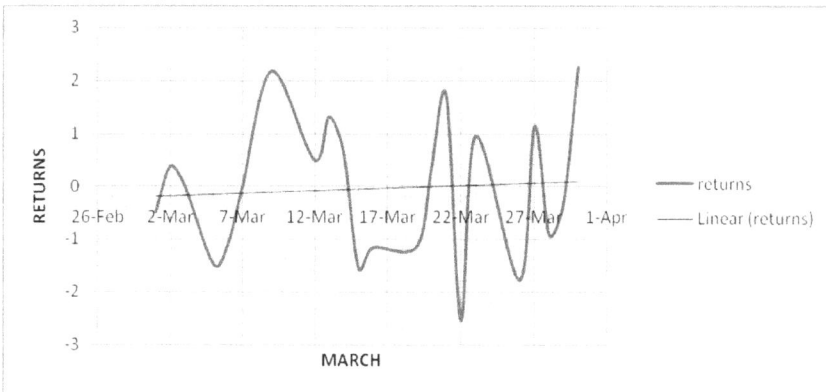

4.3.3 AUGMENTED DICKEY FULLER TEST RESULTS ON NSE RETURNS FOR THE MONTH OF MARCH 2012

Null Hypothesis: NSE RETURNS for the month of MARCH has a unit root
Exogenous: Constant
Lag Length: 1 (Fixed)

		t-Statistic	Prob.*
Augmented Dickey-Fuller test statistic		-2.808267	0.0749
Test critical values:	1% level	-3.808546	
	5% level	-3.020686	
	10% level	-2.850413	

*MacKinnon (1996) one-sided p-values.

Augmented Dickey-Fuller Test Equation
Dependent Variable: D(MARCH RETURNS)
Method: Least Squares

Sample (adjusted): 05/03/2012-30/03/2012
Included observations: 20 after adjustments

Variable	Coefficient	Std. Error	t-Statistic	Prob.
RETURNS02(-1)	-1.129432	0.402181	-2.808267	0.0121
D(RETURNS02(-1))	-0.045202	0.262138	-0.172437	0.8651
C	-0.068231	0.327009	-0.208653	0.8372

R-squared	0.552210	Mean dependent var	0.094000
Adjusted R-squared	0.499529	S.D. dependent var	2.032425
S.E. of regression	1.437818	Akaike info criterion	3.701611
Sum squared resid	35.14445	Schwarz criterion	3.850971
Log likelihood	-34.01611	Hannan-Quinn criter.	3.730768
F-statistic	10.48213	Durbin-Watson stat	1.832694
Prob(F-statistic)	0.001082		

The t-Statistic (-2.808267) is greater than the Critical Values at 1%, 5% and 10% significant levels (-3.808546, -3.020686 and -2.850413 respectively). Hence it is failed to reject the null hypothesis and it is concluded that the returns for the month of March 2012 are non-stationary.

4.4 RETURN, VARIANCE AND STANDARD DEVIATION OF NSE FOR THE MONTH OF APRIL – 2012

s.no	date	close	returns (x)	$(x - \overline{x})$	$(x - \overline{x})^2$
1	02-Apr-12	5317.9	0.41	0.45	0.20
2	03-Apr-12	5358.5	0.76	0.81	0.65
3	04-Apr-12	5322.9	-0.66	-0.62	0.39
4	09-Apr-12	5234.4	-1.66	-1.62	2.63
5	10-Apr-12	5243.6	0.18	0.22	0.05
6	11-Apr-12	5226.85	-0.32	-0.28	0.08
7	12-Apr-12	5276.85	0.96	1.00	1.00
8	13-Apr-12	5207.45	-1.32	-1.27	1.62
9	16-Apr-12	5226.2	0.36	0.40	0.16
10	17-Apr-12	5289.7	1.22	1.26	1.58
11	18-Apr-12	5300	0.19	0.24	0.06
12	19-Apr-12	5332.4	0.61	0.65	0.43
13	20-Apr-12	5290.85	-0.78	-0.74	0.54
14	23-Apr-12	5200.6	-1.71	-1.66	2.77
15	24-Apr-12	5222.65	0.42	0.47	0.22
16	25-Apr-12	5202	-0.40	-0.35	0.12
17	26-Apr-12	5189	-0.25	-0.21	0.04
18	27-Apr-12	5190.6	0.03	0.07	0.01
19	28-Apr-12	5209	0.35	0.40	0.16
20	30-Apr-12	5248.15	0.75	0.79	0.63
n = 20			$\sum x$ =-0.85		$\sum (x - \bar{x})^2 = 3.32$

DESCRIPTIVE STATISTICS	
Mean $\left(\frac{\sum x}{n}\right)$	-0.042357491
Median $\left(\frac{n+1}{2}\right)$	0.185239196
Standard Deviation $\left(\sqrt{variance}\right)$	0.816100479
Sample Variance $\left(\frac{\sum(x-\bar{x})2}{n}\right)$	0.666019993
Range	2.920807019
Minimum	-1.705775064
Maximum	1.215031954

4.4.1 JARQUE-BERA TEST :

JB (Observed value)	1.582
JB (Critical value)	5.991
DF	2
p-value	0.453
alpha	0.05

TEST INTERPRETATION:

H0: The variable from which the sample was extracted follows a Normal distribution.
Ha: The variable from which the sample was extracted does not follow a Normal distribution.
As the computed p-value is greater than the significance level alpha=0.05, one cannot
reject the null hypothesis H0.
The risk to reject the null hypothesis H0 while it is true is 45.35%.

CRITICAL VALUE:
value of the statistic under the null hypothesis for the probability 1-alpha (right-tailed test)
reject the null hypothesis when the observed value is greater than the critical value

One - tailed p-value:
probability under the null hypothesis to obtain a result as extreme as the observed
result, towards the right-tail of the distribution.
reject the null hypothesis when the probability is lower than the alpha level.

4.4.2 CONCLUSION:
At the level of significance Alpha=0.050 the decision is to not reject the null hypothesis
 that the sample follows a normal distribution.
In other words, the non-normality is not significant.

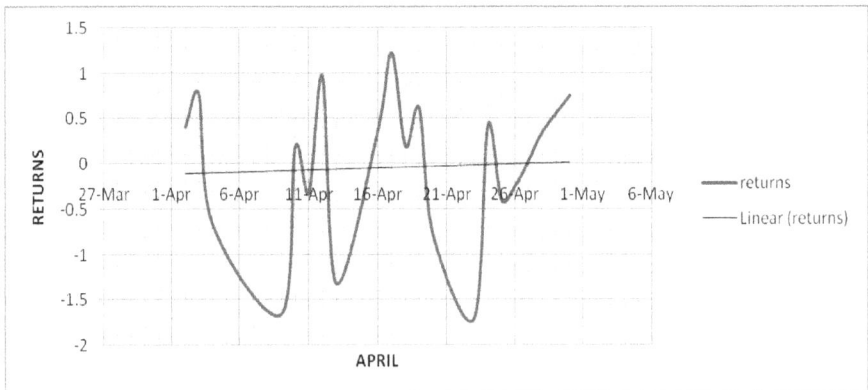

4.4.3 AUGMENTED DICKEY FULLER TEST RESULTS ON NSE RETURNS FOR THE MONTH OF APRIL 2012

Null Hypothesis: NSE RETURNS for the month of APRIL has a unit root
Exogenous: Constant
Lag Length: 1 (Fixed)

		t-Statistic	Prob.*
Augmented Dickey-Fuller test statistic		-3.429458	0.0236
Test critical values:	1% level	-3.357386	
	5% level	-3.040391	
	10% level	-2.660551	

*MacKinnon (1996) one-sided p-values.
NOTE: Probabilities and critical values calculated for 20 observations
and may not be accurate for a sample size of 18

Augmented Dickey-Fuller Test Equation
Dependent Variable: D(APRIL RETURNS)
Method: Least Squares

Sample (adjusted): 04/04/2012 - 27/04/2012
Included observations: 18 after adjustments

Variable	Coefficient	Std. Error	t-Statistic	Prob.
RETURNS03(-1)	-1.269782	0.370257	-3.429458	0.0037
D(RETURNS03(-1))	0.183396	0.252926	0.725096	0.4796
C	-0.142442	0.214060	-0.665431	0.5159

R-squared	0.552876	Mean dependent var	-0.000556
Adjusted R-squared	0.493260	S.D. dependent var	1.252238
S.E. of regression	0.891414	Akaike info criterion	2.758997
Sum squared resid	11.91929	Schwarz criterion	2.907392
Log likelihood	-21.83097	Hannan-Quinn criter.	2.779458
F-statistic	9.273877	Durbin-Watson stat	1.927660
Prob(F-statistic)	0.002389		

The t-Statistic (-3.429458) is lower than the Critical Values at 1%, 5% and 10% significant levels (-3.357386, -3.040391and -2.660551 respectively). Hence the null hypothesis is rejected and it is concluded that the returns for the month of April 2012 are stationary.

4.5 RETURN, VARIANCE AND STANDARD DEVIATION OF NSE FOR THE MONTH OF MAY – 2012

s.no	date	close	returns (x)	$(x - \bar{x})$	$(x - \bar{x})^2$
1	02-May-12	5239.15	-0.2883	0.0016	0.0000
2	03-May-12	5188.4	-0.9687	-0.6788	0.4607
3	04-May-12	5086.85	-1.9573	-1.6674	2.7801
4	07-May-12	5114.15	0.5367	0.8266	0.6832
5	08-May-12	4999.95	-2.2330	-1.9431	3.7758
6	09-May-12	4974.8	-0.5030	-0.2131	0.0454
7	10-May-12	4965.7	-0.1829	0.1070	0.0114
8	11-May-12	4928.9	-0.7411	-0.4512	0.2036
9	14-May-12	4907.8	-0.4281	-0.1382	0.0191
10	15-May-12	4942.8	0.7132	1.0030	1.0061
11	16-May-12	4858.25	-1.7106	-1.4207	2.0183
12	17-May-12	4870.2	0.2460	0.5359	0.2871
13	18-May-12	4891.45	0.4363	0.7262	0.5274
14	21-May-12	4906.05	0.2985	0.5884	0.3462
15	22-May-12	4860.5	-0.9284	-0.6386	0.4078
16	23-May-12	4835.65	-0.5113	-0.2214	0.0490
17	24-May-12	4921.4	1.7733	2.0632	4.2567
18	25-May-12	4920.4	-0.0203	0.2696	0.0727
19	28-May-12	4985.65	1.3261	1.6160	2.6115
20	29-May-12	4990.1	0.0893	0.3791	0.1438
21	30-May-12	4950.75	-0.7886	-0.4987	0.2487
22	31-May-12	4924.25	-0.5353	-0.2454	0.0602
n = 22			$\sum x$ = -6.3775		$\sum(x - \bar{x})^2$ = 20.0147

DESCRIPTIVE STATISTICS	
Mean $\left(\frac{\sum x}{n}\right)$	-0.289888192
Median $\left(\frac{n+1}{2}\right)$	-0.358211336
Standard Deviation $\left(\sqrt{variance}\right)$	0.953813107
Sample Variance $\left(\frac{\sum(x-\bar{x})2}{n}\right)$	0.909759442
Range	4.006308126
Minimum	-2.23302015
Maximum	1.773287976

4.5.1 JARQUE-BERA TEST :

JB (Observed value)	0.004
JB (Critical value)	5.991
DF	2
p-value	0.998
alpha	0.05

TEST INTERPRETATION:

H0: The variable from which the sample was extracted follows a Normal distribution.
Ha: The variable from which the sample was extracted does not follow a Normal distribution.
As the computed p-value is greater than the significance level alpha=0.05, one cannot
reject the null hypothesis H0.
The risk to reject the null hypothesis H0 while it is true is 99.78%.

CRITICAL VALUE:

value of the statistic under the null hypothesis for the probability 1-alpha (right-tailed test)
reject the null hypothesis when the observed value is greater than the critical value

One - tailed p-value:

probability under the null hypothesis to obtain a result as extreme as the observed
result, towards the right-tail of the distribution.
reject the null hypothesis when the probability is lower than the alpha level.

4.5.2 CONCLUSION:

At the level of significance Alpha=0.050 the decision is to not reject the null hypothesis
that the sample follows a normal distribution.
In other words, the non-normality is not significant.

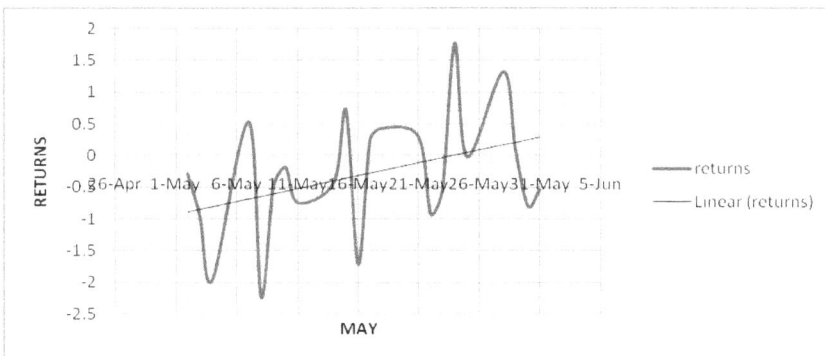

4.5.3 AUGMENTED DICKEY FULLER TEST RESULTS ON NSE RETURNS FOR THE MONTH OF MAY 2012

Null Hypothesis: NSE RETURNS for the month of MAY has a unit root
Exogenous: Constant
Lag Length: 1 (Fixed)

		t-Statistic	Prob.*
Augmented Dickey-Fuller test statistic		-2.738029	0.0853
Test critical values:	1% level	-3.808546	
	5% level	-3.020686	
	10% level	-2.750413	

*MacKinnon (1996) one-sided p-values.

Augmented Dickey-Fuller Test Equation
Dependent Variable: D(MAY RETURNS)
Method: Least Squares

Sample (adjusted): 03/05/2012 - 30/05/2012
Included observations: 20 after adjustments

Variable	Coefficient	Std. Error	t-Statistic	Prob.
RETURNS04(-1)	-0.977762	0.357105	-2.738029	0.0140
D(RETURNS04(-1))	-0.115393	0.240161	-0.480482	0.6370
C	-0.252736	0.254956	-0.991295	0.3354

R-squared	0.564297	Mean dependent var	0.021670
Adjusted R-squared	0.513037	S.D. dependent var	1.516887
S.E. of regression	1.058525	Akaike info criterion	3.089111
Sum squared resid	19.04807	Schwarz criterion	3.238471
Log likelihood	-27.89111	Hannan-Quinn criter.	3.118267
F-statistic	11.00868	Durbin-Watson stat	2.011366
Prob(F-statistic)	0.000857		

The t-Statistic (-2.738029) is greater than the Critical Values at 1%, 5% and 10% significant levels (-3.808546, -3.020686 and -2.750413 respectively). Hence it is failed to reject the null hypothesis and it is concluded that the returns for the month of May 2012 are non-stationary.

4.6 RETURN, VARIANCE AND STANDARD DEVIATION OF NSE FOR THE MONTH OF JUNE – 2012

s.no	date	close	returns (x)	$(x - \overline{x})$	$(x - \overline{x})^2$
1	01-Jun-12	4841.6	-1.4101	-1.7608	3.1005
2	04-Jun-12	4848.15	0.1353	-0.2154	0.0464
3	05-Jun-12	4863.3	0.3125	-0.0382	0.0015
4	06-Jun-12	4997.1	2.7512	2.4006	5.7626
5	07-Jun-12	5049.65	1.0516	0.7009	0.4913
6	08-Jun-12	5068.35	0.3703	0.0197	0.0004
7	11-Jun-12	5054.1	-0.2812	-0.6318	0.3992
8	12-Jun-12	5115.9	1.2228	0.8721	0.7606
9	13-Jun-12	5121.45	0.1085	-0.2422	0.0587
10	14-Jun-12	5054.75	-1.3024	-1.6530	2.7325
11	15-Jun-12	5139.05	1.6677	1.3171	1.7347
12	18-Jun-12	5064.25	-1.4555	-1.8062	3.2623
13	19-Jun-12	5103.85	0.7820	0.4313	0.1860
14	20-Jun-12	5120.55	0.3272	-0.0235	0.0006
15	21-Jun-12	5165	0.8681	0.5174	0.2677
16	22-Jun-12	5146.05	-0.3669	-0.7176	0.5149
17	25-Jun-12	5114.65	-0.6102	-0.9608	0.9232
18	26-Jun-12	5120.8	0.1202	-0.2304	0.0531
19	27-Jun-12	5141.9	0.4120	0.0614	0.0038
20	28-Jun-12	5149.15	0.1410	-0.2097	0.0440
21	29-Jun-12	5278.9	2.5198	2.1692	4.7053
n = 21			$\sum x = 7.3640$		$\sum(x - \bar{x})^2 =$ 25.0491

DESCRIPTIVE STATISTICS	
Mean $\left(\frac{\sum x}{n}\right)$	0.350667167
Median $\left(\frac{n+1}{2}\right)$	0.312490331
Standard Deviation $\left(\sqrt{variance}\right)$	1.092159547
Sample Variance $\left(\frac{\sum(x-\bar{x})2}{n}\right)$	1.192812477
Range	4.206740244
Minimum	-1.455521935
Maximum	2.751218309

4.6.1 JARQUE-BERA TEST :

JB (Observed value)	0.481
JB (Critical value)	5.991
DF	2
p-value	0.786
alpha	0.05

TEST INTERPRETATION:

H0: The variable from which the sample was extracted follows a Normal distribution.
Ha: The variable from which the sample was extracted does not follow a Normal distribution.
As the computed p-value is greater than the significance level alpha=0.05, one cannot
reject the null hypothesis H0.
The risk to reject the null hypothesis H0 while it is true is 78.60%.

CRITICAL VALUE:
value of the statistic under the null hypothesis for the probability 1-alpha (right-tailed test)
reject the null hypothesis when the observed value is greater than the critical value

One - tailed p-value:
probability under the null hypothesis to obtain a result as extreme as the observed
result, towards the right-tail of the distribution.
reject the null hypothesis when the probability is lower than the alpha level.

4.6.2 CONCLUSION:
At the level of significance Alpha=0.050 the decision is to not reject the null hypothesis
that the sample follows a normal distribution.
In other words, the non-normality is not significant.

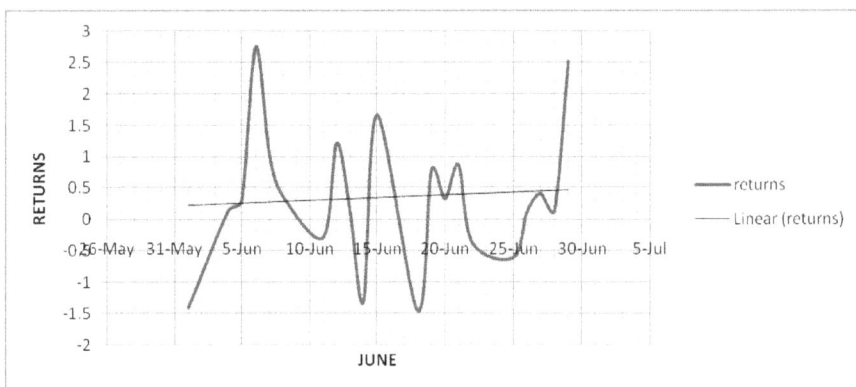

4.6.3 AUGMENTED DICKEY FULLER TEST RESULTS ON NSE RETURNS FOR THE MONTH OF JUNE 2012

Null Hypothesis: NSE RETURNS for the month of JUNE has a unit root
Exogenous: Constant
Lag Length: 1 (Fixed)

		t-Statistic	Prob.*
Augmented Dickey-Fuller test statistic		-2.906162	0.0632
Test critical values:	1% level	-3.831511	
	5% level	-3.029970	
	10% level	-2.955194	

*MacKinnon (1996) one-sided p-values.
NOTE: Probabilities and critical values calculated for 20 observations
      and may not be accurate for a sample size of 19

Augmented Dickey-Fuller Test Equation
Dependent Variable: D(JUNE RETURNS)
Method: Least Squares

Sample (adjusted): 05/06/2012 - 29/06/2012
Included observations: 19 after adjustments

Variable	Coefficient	Std. Error	t-Statistic	Prob.
RETURNS05(-1)	-1.196160	0.411594	-2.906162	0.0103
D(RETURNS05(-1))	-0.031095	0.257980	-0.120533	0.9056
C	0.521777	0.287699	1.813619	0.0885

R-squared	0.558402	Mean dependent var	0.125500
Adjusted R-squared	0.503202	S.D. dependent var	1.615341
S.E. of regression	1.138555	Akaike info criterion	3.241336
Sum squared resid	20.74093	Schwarz criterion	3.390458
Log likelihood	-27.79270	Hannan-Quinn criter.	3.266574
F-statistic	10.11601	Durbin-Watson stat	1.798624
Prob(F-statistic)	0.001446		

The t-Statistic (-2.906162) is greater than the Critical Values at 1%, 5% and 10% significant levels (-3.831511, -3.029970 and -2.955194 respectively). Hence it is failed to reject the null hypothesis and it is concluded that the returns for the month of June 2012 are non-stationary.

4.7 RETURN, VARIANCE AND STANDARD DEVIATION OF NSE FOR THE MONTH OF JULY – 2011

s.no	date	close	returns (x)	$(x - \overline{x})$	$(x - \overline{x})^2$
1	02-Jul-12	5278.6	-0.0994	-0.0557	0.0031
2	03-Jul-12	5287.95	0.1771	0.2208	0.0488
3	04-Jul-12	5302.55	0.2761	0.3198	0.1023
4	05-Jul-12	5327.3	0.4668	0.5104	0.2605
5	06-Jul-12	5316.95	-0.1943	-0.1506	0.0227
6	09-Jul-12	5275.15	-0.7862	-0.7425	0.5513
7	10-Jul-12	5345.35	1.3308	1.3744	1.8891
8	11-Jul-12	5306.3	-0.7305	-0.6869	0.4718
9	12-Jul-12	5235.25	-1.3390	-1.2953	1.6778
10	13-Jul-12	5227.25	-0.1528	-0.1091	0.0119
11	16-Jul-12	5197.25	-0.5739	-0.5302	0.2812
12	17-Jul-12	5192.85	-0.0847	-0.0410	0.0017
13	18-Jul-12	5216.3	0.4516	0.4953	0.2453
14	19-Jul-12	5242.7	0.5061	0.5498	0.3023
15	20-Jul-12	5205.1	-0.7172	-0.6735	0.4536
16	23-Jul-12	5117.95	-1.6743	-1.6306	2.6590
17	24-Jul-12	5128.2	0.2003	0.2440	0.0595
18	25-Jul-12	5109.6	-0.3627	-0.3190	0.1018
19	26-Jul-12	5043	-1.3034	-1.2598	1.5870
20	27-Jul-12	5099.85	1.1273	1.1710	1.3712
21	30-Jul-12	5199.8	1.9599	2.0035	4.0142
22	31-Jul-12	5229	0.5616	0.6052	0.3663
n=22			$\sum x = -0.9609$		$\sum(x - \overline{x})^2 =$ 16.4821

DESCRIPTIVE STATISTICS	
Mean $\left(\frac{\sum x}{n}\right)$	-0.043677278
Median $\left(\frac{n+1}{2}\right)$	-0.092009763
Standard Deviation $\left(\sqrt{variance}\right)$	0.865556613
Sample Variance $\left(\frac{\sum(x-\bar{x})2}{n}\right)$	0.749188251
Range	3.634180982
Minimum	-1.674319417
Maximum	1.959861565

4.7.1 JARQUE-BERA TEST :

JB (Observed value)	0.207
JB (Critical value)	5.991
DF	2
p-value	0.902
alpha	0.05

TEST INTERPRETATION:

H0: The variable from which the sample was extracted follows a Normal distribution.
Ha: The variable from which the sample was extracted does not follow a Normal distribution.
As the computed p-value is greater than the significance level alpha=0.05, one cannot
 reject the null hypothesis H0.
The risk to reject the null hypothesis H0 while it is true is 90.16%.

CRITICAL VALUE:
value of the statistic under the null hypothesis for the probability 1-alpha (right-tailed test)
reject the null hypothesis when the observed value is greater than the critical value

One - tailed p-value:
probability under the null hypothesis to obtain a result as extreme as the observed result,
towards the right-tail of the distribution.
reject the null hypothesis when the probability is lower than the alpha level.

4.7.2 CONCLUSION:
At the level of significance Alpha=0.050 the decision is to not reject the null hypothesis
 that the sample follows a normal distribution.

In other words, the non-normality is not significant.

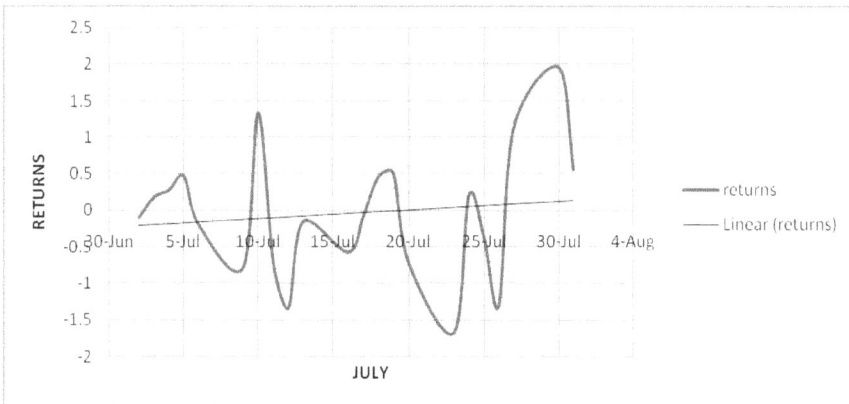

4.7.3 AUGMENTED DICKEY FULLER TEST RESULTS ON NSE RETURNS FOR THE MONTH OF JULY 2012

Null Hypothesis: NSE RETURNS for the month of JULY has a unit root
Exogenous: Constant
Lag Length: 1 (Fixed)

		t-Statistic	Prob.*
Augmented Dickey-Fuller test statistic		-3.697731	0.0126
Test critical values:	1% level	-3.608546	
	5% level	-3.020686	
	10% level	-2.650413	

*MacKinnon (1996) one-sided p-values.

Augmented Dickey-Fuller Test Equation
Dependent Variable: D(JULY RETURNS)
Method: Least Squares

Sample (adjusted): 04/07/2012 - 31/07/2012
Included observations: 20 after adjustments

Variable	Coefficient	Std. Error	t-Statistic	Prob.
RETURNS06(-1)	-1.240231	0.335403	-3.697731	0.0018
D(RETURNS06(-1))	0.418110	0.265745	1.573351	0.1341
C	-0.112068	0.208668	-0.537065	0.5982

R-squared	0.494040	Mean dependent var	0.019225
Adjusted R-squared	0.434516	S.D. dependent var	1.208014
S.E. of regression	0.908411	Akaike info criterion	2.783242
Sum squared resid	14.02858	Schwarz criterion	2.932601
Log likelihood	-24.83242	Hannan-Quinn criter.	2.812398
F-statistic	8.299756	Durbin-Watson stat	1.832396
Prob(F-statistic)	0.003055		

The t-Statistic (-3.697731) is lower than the Critical Values at 1%, 5% and 10% significant levels (-3.608546, -3.020686 and -2.650413 respectively). Hence the null hypothesis is rejected and it is concluded that the returns for the month of July 2012 are stationary.

4.8 RETURN, VARIANCE AND STANDARD DEVIATION OF NASDAQ FOR THE MONTH OF JANUARY – 2012

s.no	date	close	returns (x)	$(x - \bar{x})$	$(x - \bar{x})^2$
1	03-01-12	24.96	1.84	1.78	3.15
2	04-01-12	24.62	-1.36	-1.42	2.02
3	05-01-12	24.66	0.16	0.10	0.01
4	06-01-12	24.43	-0.93	-0.99	0.99
5	09-01-12	24.33	-0.41	-0.47	0.22
6	10-01-12	25.17	3.45	3.39	11.51
7	11-01-12	25.05	-0.48	-0.54	0.29
8	12-01-12	24.96	-0.36	-0.42	0.18
9	13-01-12	24.8	-0.64	-0.70	0.49
10	17-01-12	24.52	-1.13	-1.19	1.41
11	18-01-12	24.78	1.06	1.00	1.00
12	19-01-12	25.14	1.45	1.39	1.94
13	20-01-12	25.34	0.80	0.74	0.54
14	23-01-12	25.46	0.47	0.41	0.17
15	24-01-12	25.66	0.79	0.73	0.53
16	25-01-12	25.9	0.94	0.88	0.77
17	26-01-12	25.83	-0.27	-0.33	0.11
18	27-01-12	25.99	0.62	0.56	0.31
19	30-01-12	25.3	-2.65	-2.72	7.37
20	31-01-12	24.76	-2.13	-2.19	4.82
n = 20			$\sum x = 1.20$		$\sum(x - \bar{x})^2 = 37.82$

DESCRIPTIVE STATISTICS	
Mean $\left(\frac{\sum x}{n}\right)$	0.060185004
Median $\left(\frac{n+1}{2}\right)$	-0.053900367
Standard Deviation $\left(\sqrt{variance}\right)$	1.375216161
Sample Variance $\left(\frac{\sum(x-\bar{x})2}{n}\right)$	1.891219489
Range	6.107395
Minimum	-2.654867257
Maximum	3.452527744

4.8.1 JARQUE-BERA TEST:

JB (observed value)	1.185
JB (critical value)	5.991
DF	2
One-tailed p-value	0.553
Alpha	0.05

TEST
INTERPRETATION:

H0: The variable from which the sample was extracted follows a Normal distribution.
Ha: The variable from which the sample was extracted does not follow a Normal distribution.
As the computed p-value is greater than the significance level alpha=0.05, one cannot reject the null hypothesis H0.
The risk to reject the null hypothesis H0 while it is true is 55.31%.

CRITICAL VALUE:
value of the statistic under the null hypothesis for the probability 1-alpha (right-tailed test)
reject the null hypothesis when the observed value is greater than the critical value

One - tailed p-value:
probability under the null hypothesis to obtain a result as extreme as the observed result, towards the right-tail of the distribution.
reject the null hypothesis when the probability is lower than the alpha level.

4.8.2 CONCLUSION:
At the level of significance Alpha=0.050 the decision is to not reject the null hypothesis that the sample follows a normal distribution.
In other words, the non-normality is not significant.

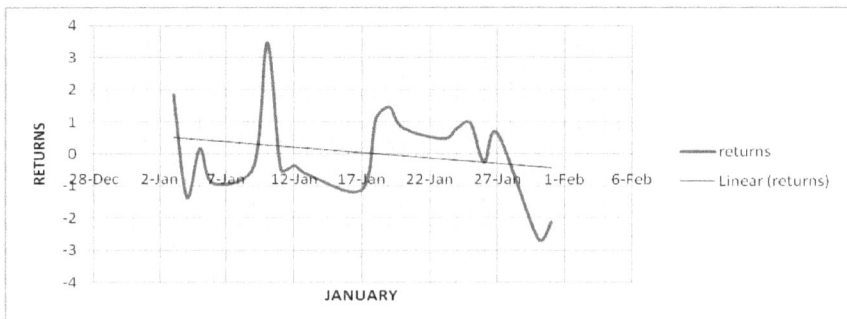

4.8.3 AUGMENTED DICKEY FULLER TEST RESULTS ON NASDAQ RETURNS FOR THE MONTH OF JANUARY 2012

Null Hypothesis: NASDAQ RETURNS for the month of JANUARY has a unit root
Exogenous: Constant
Lag Length: 1 (Fixed)

		t-Statistic	Prob.*
Augmented Dickey-Fuller test statistic		-1.807166	0.3638
Test critical values:	1% level	-3.920350	
	5% level	-3.065585	
	10% level	-2.673459	

*MacKinnon (1996) one-sided p-values.
NOTE: Probabilities and critical values calculated for 20 observations
and may not be accurate for a sample size of 16

Augmented Dickey-Fuller Test Equation
Dependent Variable: D(JANUARY RETURNS)
Method: Least Squares

Sample (adjusted): 05/01/2012 - 31/01/2012
Included observations: 16 after adjustments

Variable	Coefficient	Std. Error	t-Statistic	Prob.
RETURNS(-1)	-0.878286	0.486002	-1.807166	0.0939
D(RETURNS(-1))	0.047591	0.323955	0.146905	0.8855
C	0.036738	0.410272	0.089547	0.9300

R-squared	0.388944	Mean dependent var	-0.154375
Adjusted R-squared	0.294935	S.D. dependent var	1.786109
S.E. of regression	1.499763	Akaike info criterion	3.815852
Sum squared resid	29.24075	Schwarz criterion	3.960712
Log likelihood	-27.52681	Hannan-Quinn criter.	3.823270
F-statistic	4.137317	Durbin-Watson stat	2.015002
Prob(F-statistic)	0.040694		

The t-Statistic (-1.807166) is greater than the Critical Values at 1%, 5% and 10% significant levels (-3.920350, -3.065585 and -2.673459 respectively). Hence it is failed to reject the null hypothesis and it is concluded that the returns for the month of January 2012 are non-stationary.

4.9 RETURN, VARIANCE AND STANDARD DEVIATION OF NASDAQ FOR THE MONTH OF FEBRUARY – 2012

s.no	date	close	returns (x)	$(x - \bar{x})$	$(x - \bar{x})^2$
1	01-02-12	24.77	0.04	-0.28	0.08
2	02-02-12	24.66	-0.44	-0.76	0.58
3	03-02-12	25.07	1.66	1.35	1.81
4	06-02-12	25.35	1.12	0.80	0.64
5	07-02-12	25.7	1.38	1.06	1.13
6	08-02-12	26.24	2.10	1.79	3.19
7	09-02-12	25.88	-1.37	-1.69	2.85
8	10-02-12	26	0.46	0.15	0.02
9	13-02-12	26.36	1.38	1.07	1.14
10	14-02-12	26.36	0.00	-0.32	0.10
11	15-02-12	26.21	-0.57	-0.88	0.78
12	16-02-12	26.75	2.06	1.74	3.04
13	17-02-12	26.81	0.22	-0.09	0.01
14	21-02-12	26.6	-0.78	-1.10	1.21
15	22-02-12	26.22	-1.43	-1.74	3.04
16	23-02-12	26.26	0.15	-0.16	0.03
17	24-02-12	26.69	1.64	1.32	1.75
18	27-02-12	26.79	0.37	0.06	0.00
19	28-02-12	26.63	-0.60	-0.91	0.83
20	29-02-12	26.34	-1.09	-1.40	1.97
N =20			$\sum x = 6.32$		$\sum(x - \bar{x})^2 = 24.21$

DESCRIPTIVE STATISTICS	
Mean $\left(\frac{\sum x}{n}\right)$	0.315805346
Median $\left(\frac{n+1}{2}\right)$	0.188427183
Standard Deviation $\left(\sqrt{variance}\right)$	1.100278255
Sample Variance $\left(\frac{\sum(x-\bar{x})2}{n}\right)$	1.210612239
Range	3.529738744
Minimum	-1.428571429
Maximum	2.101167315

4.9.1 JARQUE-BERA TEST:

JB (observed value)	1.204
JB (critical value)	5.991
DF	2
One-tailed p-value	0.548
Alpha	0.05

TEST INTERPRETATION:

H0: The variable from which the sample was extracted follows a Normal distribution.
Ha: The variable from which the sample was extracted does not follow a Normal distribution.
As the computed p-value is greater than the significance level alpha=0.05, one cannot
reject the null hypothesis H0.
The risk to reject the null hypothesis H0 while it is true is 54.80%.

CRITICAL VALUE:
value of the statistic under the null hypothesis for the probability 1-alpha (right-tailed test)
reject the null hypothesis when the observed value is greater than the critical value

One - tailed p-value:
probability under the null hypothesis to obtain a result as extreme as the observed result,
towards the right-tail of the distribution.
reject the null hypothesis when the probability is lower than the alpha level.

4.9.2 CONCLUSION:
At the level of significance Alpha=0.050 the decision is to not reject the null hypothesis
that the sample follows a normal distribution.
In other words, the non-normality is not significant.

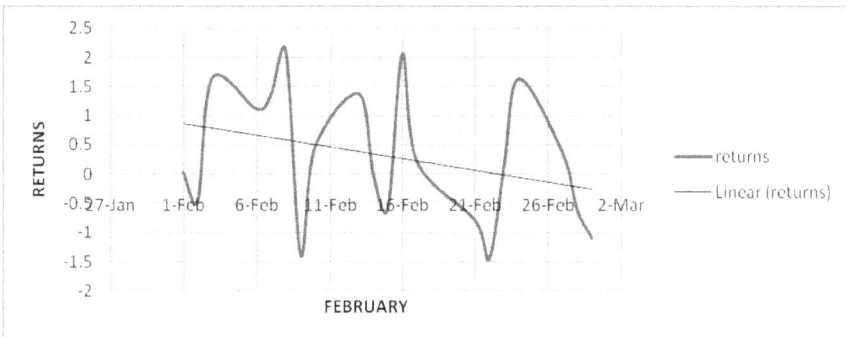

4.9.3 AUGMENTED DICKEY FULLER TEST RESULTS ON NASDAQ RETURNS FOR THE MONTH OF FEBRUARY 2012

Null Hypothesis: NASDAQ RETURNS for the month of FEBRUARY has a unit root
Exogenous: Constant
Lag Length: 1 (Fixed)

		t-Statistic	Prob.*
Augmented Dickey-Fuller test statistic		-3.765181	0.0121
Test critical values:	1% level	-3.857386	
	5% level	-3.040391	
	10% level	-2.660551	

*MacKinnon (1996) one-sided p-values.
NOTE: Probabilities and critical values calculated for 20 observations
    and may not be accurate for a sample size of 18

Augmented Dickey-Fuller Test Equation
Dependent Variable: D(FEBRUARY RETURNS)
Method: Least Squares

Sample (adjusted): 03/02/2012 - 28/02/2012
Included observations: 18 after adjustments

Variable	Coefficient	Std. Error	t-Statistic	Prob.
RETURNS01(-1)	-1.330856	0.353464	-3.765181	0.0019
D(RETURNS01(-1))	0.389076	0.252892	1.538510	0.1447
C	0.521156	0.312537	1.667503	0.1162

R-squared	0.529222	Mean dependent var	-0.036111
Adjusted R-squared	0.466452	S.D. dependent var	1.589766
S.E. of regression	1.161235	Akaike info criterion	3.287856
Sum squared resid	20.22699	Schwarz criterion	3.436252
Log likelihood	-26.59071	Hannan-Quinn criter.	3.308318
F-statistic	8.431078	Durbin-Watson stat	1.754379
Prob(F-statistic)	0.003517		

The t-Statistic (-3.765181) is greater than the Critical Values at 1% significance level (-3.857386) and lower than 5% and 10% significant levels (-3.040391 and -2.660551 respectively). Hence it is failed to reject the null hypothesis and it is concluded that the returns for the month of February 2012 are non-stationary.

4.10 RETURN, VARIANCE AND STANDARD DEVIATION OF NASDAQ FOR THE MONTH OF MARCH – 2012

s.no	date	close	returns (x)	$(x - \bar{x})$	$(x - \bar{x})^2$
1	01-03-12	26.31	-0.11	-0.05	0.00
2	02-03-12	26.11	-0.76	-0.69	0.48
3	05-03-12	26.15	0.15	0.22	0.05
4	06-03-12	25.47	-2.60	-2.53	6.42
5	07-03-12	25.64	0.67	0.73	0.54
6	08-03-12	25.95	1.21	1.28	1.63
7	09-03-12	26.13	0.69	0.76	0.58
8	12-03-12	25.84	-1.11	-1.04	1.09
9	13-03-12	26.72	3.41	3.47	12.06
10	14-03-12	26.49	-0.86	-0.79	0.63
11	15-03-12	26.75	0.98	1.05	1.10
12	16-03-12	26.61	-0.52	-0.46	0.21
13	19-03-12	26.8	0.71	0.78	0.61
14	20-03-12	26.72	-0.30	-0.23	0.05
15	21-03-12	26.85	0.49	0.55	0.31
16	22-03-12	26.88	0.11	0.18	0.03
17	23-03-12	26.64	-0.89	-0.83	0.68
18	26-03-12	27.18	2.03	2.09	4.39
19	27-03-12	26.61	-2.10	-2.03	4.12
20	28-03-12	26.42	-0.71	-0.65	0.42
21	29-03-12	25.82	-2.27	-2.20	4.86
22	30-03-12	25.9	0.31	0.38	0.14
n = 22			$\sum x = -1.48$		$\sum(x - \bar{x})^2 = 40.39$

DESCRIPTIVE STATISTICS	
Mean $\left(\frac{\sum x}{n}\right)$	-0.067381211
Median $\left(\frac{n+1}{2}\right)$	-0.001081686
Standard Deviation $\left(\sqrt{variance}\right)$	1.35492511
Sample Variance $\left(\frac{\sum(x-\bar{x})2}{n}\right)$	1.835822053
Range	6.005955165
Minimum	-2.600382409
Maximum	3.405572755

4.10.1 JARQUE-BERA TEST:

JB (observed value)	0.546
JB (critical value)	5.991
DF	2
One-tailed p-value	0.761
Alpha	0.05

TEST INTERPRETATION:

H0: The variable from which the sample was extracted follows a Normal distribution.
Ha: The variable from which the sample was extracted does not follow a Normal distribution.
As the computed p-value is greater than the significance level alpha=0.05, one cannot
reject the null hypothesis H0.
The risk to reject the null hypothesis H0 while it is true is 76.12%.

CRITICAL VALUE:
value of the statistic under the null hypothesis for the probability 1-alpha (right-tailed test)
reject the null hypothesis when the observed value is greater than the critical value

One - tailed p-value:
probability under the null hypothesis to obtain a result as extreme as the observed result,
towards the right-tail of the distribution.
reject the null hypothesis when the probability is lower than the alpha level.

4.10.2 CONCLUSION:
At the level of significance Alpha=0.050 the decision is to not reject the null hypothesis
that the sample follows a normal distribution.
In other words, the non-normality is not significant.

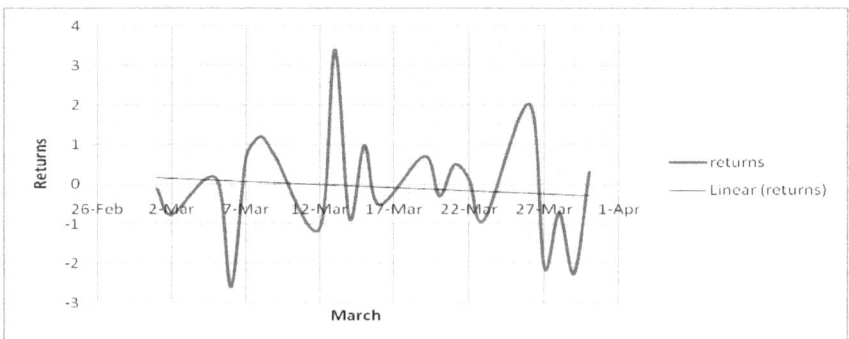

4.10.3 AUGMENTED DICKEY FULLER TEST RESULTS ON NASDAQ RETURNS FOR THE MONTH OF MARCH 2012

Null Hypothesis: NASDAQ RETURNS for the month of MARCH has a unit root
Exogenous: Constant
Lag Length: 1 (Fixed)

		t-Statistic	Prob.*
Augmented Dickey-Fuller test statistic		-2.654584	0.0993
Test critical values:	1% level	-3.808546	
	5% level	-3.020686	
	10% level	-2.656413	

*MacKinnon (1996) one-sided p-values.

Augmented Dickey-Fuller Test Equation
Dependent Variable: D(MARCH RETURNS)
Method: Least Squares

Sample (adjusted): 05/03/2012 - 30/03/2012
Included observations: 20 after adjustments

Variable	Coefficient	Std. Error	t-Statistic	Prob.
RETURNS02(-1)	-1.066060	0.401592	-2.654584	0.0167
D(RETURNS02(-1))	-0.211378	0.252790	-0.836180	0.4147
C	-0.058345	0.315381	-0.184998	0.8554

R-squared	0.688050	Mean dependent var	0.053500
Adjusted R-squared	0.651350	S.D. dependent var	2.384534
S.E. of regression	1.407986	Akaike info criterion	3.659679
Sum squared resid	33.70122	Schwarz criterion	3.809039
Log likelihood	-33.59679	Hannan-Quinn criter.	3.688835
F-statistic	18.74796	Durbin-Watson stat	1.995228
Prob(F-statistic)	0.000050		

The t-Statistic (-2.654584) is greater than the Critical Values at 1%, 5% and 10% significant levels (-3.808546, -3.020686 and -2.656413 respectively). Hence it is failed to reject the null hypothesis and it is concluded that the returns for the month of March 2012 are non-stationary.

4.11 RETURN, VARIANCE AND STANDARD DEVIATION OF NASDAQ FOR THE MONTH OF APRIL – 2012

s.no	date	close	returns (x)	$(x - \bar{x})$	$(x - \bar{x})^2$
1	02-04-12	25.93	0.12	0.37	0.14
2	03-04-12	25.73	-0.77	-0.52	0.27
3	04-04-12	25.22	-1.98	-1.73	2.98
4	05-04-12	25.52	1.19	1.45	2.09
5	09-04-12	25.35	-0.67	-0.41	0.17
6	10-04-12	24.59	-3.00	-2.74	7.52
7	11-04-12	24.73	0.57	0.83	0.68
8	12-04-12	24.95	0.89	1.15	1.31
9	13-04-12	24.57	-1.52	-1.27	1.61
10	16-04-12	24.43	-0.57	-0.31	0.10
11	17-04-12	24.78	1.43	1.69	2.85
12	18-04-12	24.71	-0.28	-0.03	0.00
13	19-04-12	24.7	-0.04	0.22	0.05
14	20-04-12	25.04	1.38	1.63	2.66
15	23-04-12	25.02	-0.08	0.18	0.03
16	24-04-12	25.33	1.24	1.49	2.23
17	25-04-12	25.12	-0.83	-0.57	0.33
18	26-04-12	25.07	-0.20	0.06	0.00
19	27-04-12	25.14	0.28	0.54	0.29
20	30-04-12	24.57	-2.27	-2.01	4.05
n = 20			$\sum x$ = -5.12		$\sum (x - \bar{x})^2$ = 29.35

DESCRIPTIVE STATISTICS	
Mean $\left(\frac{\sum x}{n}\right)$	-0.255848123
Median $\left(\frac{n+1}{2}\right)$	-0.139458395
Standard Deviation $\left(\sqrt{variance}\right)$	1.211417268
Sample Variance $\left(\frac{\sum(x-\bar{x})2}{n}\right)$	1.467531798
Range	4.43069237
Minimum	-2.998027613
Maximum	1.432664756

4.11.1 JARQUE-BERA TEST:

JB (observed value)	1.049
JB (critical value)	5.991
DF	2
One-tailed p-value	0.592
Alpha	0.05

TEST INTERPRETATION:

H0: The variable from which the sample was extracted follows a Normal distribution.
Ha: The variable from which the sample was extracted does not follow a Normal distribution.
As the computed p-value is greater than the significance level alpha=0.05, one cannot
reject the null hypothesis H0.
The risk to reject the null hypothesis H0 while it is true is 59.21%.

CRITICAL VALUE:
value of the statistic under the null hypothesis for the probability 1-alpha (right-tailed test)
reject the null hypothesis when the observed value is greater than the critical value

One - tailed p-value:
probability under the null hypothesis to obtain a result as extreme as the observed result,
towards the right-tail of the distribution.
reject the null hypothesis when the probability is lower than the alpha level.

4.11.2 CONCLUSION:
At the level of significance Alpha=0.050 the decision is to not reject the null hypothesis
that the sample follows a normal distribution.
In other words, the non-normality is not significant.

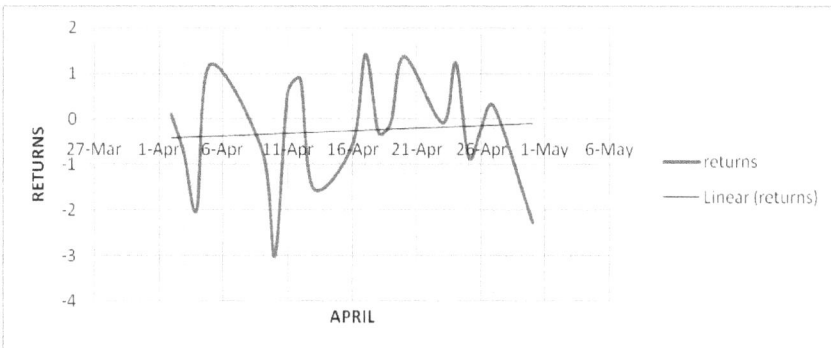

4.11.3 AUGMENTED DICKEY FULLER TEST RESULTS ON NASDAQ RETURNS FOR THE MONTH OF APRIL 2012

Null Hypothesis: NASDAQ RETURNS for the month of APRIL has a unit root
Exogenous: Constant
Lag Length: 1 (Fixed)

		t-Statistic	Prob.*
Augmented Dickey-Fuller test statistic		-4.339425	0.0038
Test critical values:	1% level	-3.857386	
	5% level	-3.040391	
	10% level	-2.660551	

*MacKinnon (1996) one-sided p-values.
NOTE: Probabilities and critical values calculated for 20 observations
    and may not be accurate for a sample size of 18

Augmented Dickey-Fuller Test Equation
Dependent Variable: D(APRIL RETURNS)
Method: Least Squares

Sample (adjusted): 4/04/2012 - 4/27/2012
Included observations: 18 after adjustments

Variable	Coefficient	Std. Error	t-Statistic	Prob.
RETURNS03(-1)	-1.695574	0.390737	-4.339425	0.0006
D(RETURNS03(-1))	0.420819	0.255483	1.647155	0.1203
C	-0.365902	0.303301	-1.206400	0.2463

R-squared	0.630994	Mean dependent var	-0.083333
Adjusted R-squared	0.581793	S.D. dependent var	1.942121
S.E. of regression	1.255949	Akaike info criterion	3.444672
Sum squared resid	23.66112	Schwarz criterion	3.593067
Log likelihood	-28.00205	Hannan-Quinn criter.	3.465133
F-statistic	12.82486	Durbin-Watson stat	1.391830
Prob(F-statistic)	0.000566		

The t-Statistic (-4.339425) is lower than the Critical Values at 1%, 5% and 10% significant levels (-3.857386, -3.040391and -2.660551respectively). Hence the null hypothesis is rejected and it is concluded that the returns for the month of April 2012 are stationary.

4.12 RETURN, VARIANCE AND STANDARD DEVIATION OF NASDAQ FOR THE MONTH OF MAY – 2012

s.no	date	close	returns (x)	$(x - \bar{x})$	$(x - \bar{x})^2$
1	01-05-12	24.44	-0.53	-0.02	0.00
2	02-05-12	24.09	-1.43	-0.92	0.85
3	03-05-12	23.67	-1.74	-1.23	1.52
4	04-05-12	23.67	0.00	0.51	0.26
5	07-05-12	23.44	-0.97	-0.46	0.21
6	08-05-12	23.65	0.90	1.41	1.98
7	09-05-12	24.06	1.73	2.25	5.04
8	10-05-12	23.73	-1.37	-0.86	0.74
9	11-05-12	23.36	-1.56	-1.05	1.10
10	14-05-12	23.56	0.86	1.37	1.87
11	15-05-12	23.68	0.51	1.02	1.04
12	16-05-12	23.115	-2.39	-1.87	3.51
13	17-05-12	23	-0.50	0.01	0.00
14	18-05-12	21.99	-4.39	-3.88	15.05
15	21-05-12	22.78	3.59	4.10	16.84
16	22-05-12	22.32	-2.02	-1.51	2.27
17	23-05-12	21.81	-2.28	-1.77	3.15
18	24-05-12	21.8	-0.05	0.47	0.22
19	25-05-12	22.06	1.19	1.70	2.90
20	29-05-12	22.22	0.73	1.24	1.53
21	30-05-12	21.81	-1.85	-1.33	1.78
22	31-05-12	21.88	0.32	0.83	0.69
n = 22			$\sum x$ = -11.25		$\sum(x - \bar{x})^2$ = 62.56

DESCRIPTIVE STATISTICS	
Mean $\left(\frac{\sum x}{n}\right)$	-0.511397008
Median $\left(\frac{n+1}{2}\right)$	-0.513306483
Standard Deviation $\left(\sqrt{variance}\right)$	1.686324045
Sample Variance $\left(\frac{\sum(x-\bar{x})2}{n}\right)$	2.843688784
Range	7.983846412
Minimum	-4.391304348
Maximum	3.592542065

4.12.1 JARQUE-BERA TEST:

JB (observed value)	0.156
JB (critical value)	5.991
DF	2
One-tailed p-value	0.925
Alpha	0.05

TEST INTERPRETATION:

H0: The variable from which the sample was extracted follows a Normal distribution.
Ha: The variable from which the sample was extracted does not follow a Normal distribution.
As the computed p-value is greater than the significance level alpha=0.05, one cannot reject the null hypothesis H0.
The risk to reject the null hypothesis H0 while it is true is 55.31%.

CRITICAL VALUE:
value of the statistic under the null hypothesis for the probability 1-alpha (right-tailed test)
reject the null hypothesis when the observed value is greater than the critical value

One - tailed p-value:
probability under the null hypothesis to obtain a result as extreme as the observed result, towards the right-tail of the distribution.
reject the null hypothesis when the probability is lower than the alpha level.

4.12.2 CONCLUSION:
At the level of significance Alpha=0.050 the decision is to not reject the null hypothesis that the sample follows a normal distribution.
In other words, the non-normality is not significant.

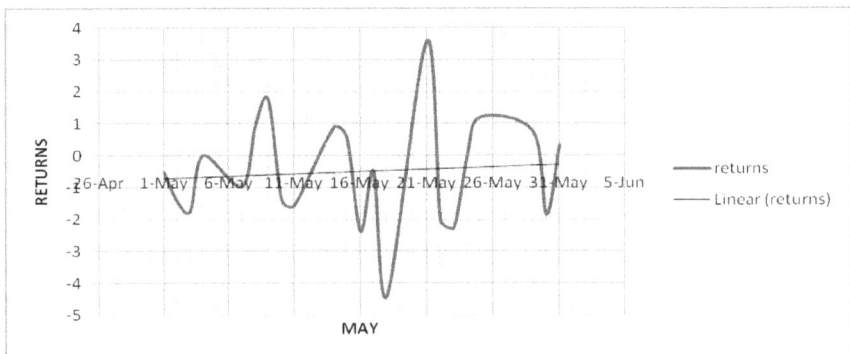

4.12.3 AUGMENTED DICKEY FULLER TEST RESULTS ON NASDAQ RETURNS FOR THE MONTH OF MAY 2012

Null Hypothesis: NASDAQ RETURNS for the month of MAY has a unit root
Exogenous: Constant
Lag Length: 1 (Fixed)

		t-Statistic	Prob.*
Augmented Dickey-Fuller test statistic		-4.330763	0.0033
Test critical values:	1% level	-3.808546	
	5% level	-3.020686	
	10% level	-2.650413	

*MacKinnon (1996) one-sided p-values.

Augmented Dickey-Fuller Test Equation
Dependent Variable: D(MAY RETURNS)
Method: Least Squares

Sample (adjusted): 03/05/2012 - 30/05/2012
Included observations: 20 after adjustments

Variable	Coefficient	Std. Error	t-Statistic	Prob.
RETURNS04(-1)	-1.653461	0.381794	-4.330763	0.0005
D(RETURNS04(-1))	0.247313	0.237066	1.043225	0.3115
C	-0.808888	0.437235	-1.850008	0.0818

R-squared	0.685397	Mean dependent var	0.087500
Adjusted R-squared	0.648385	S.D. dependent var	2.939244
S.E. of regression	1.742888	Akaike info criterion	4.086445
Sum squared resid	51.64021	Schwarz criterion	4.235805
Log likelihood	-37.86445	Hannan-Quinn criter.	4.115602
F-statistic	18.51817	Durbin-Watson stat	2.113766
Prob(F-statistic)	0.000054		

The t-Statistic (-4.330763) is lower than the Critical Values at 1%, 5% and 10% significant levels (-3.808546, -3.020686 and -2.650413 respectively). Hence the null hypothesis is rejected and it is concluded that the returns for the month of May 2012 are stationary.

4.13 RETURN, VARIANCE AND STANDARD DEVIATION OF NASDAQ FOR THE MONTH OF JUNE – 2012

s.no	date	close	returns (x)	$(x - \bar{x})$	$(x - \bar{x})^2$
1	01-06-12	21.38	-2.29	-2.47	6.10
2	04-06-12	21.39	0.05	-0.14	0.02
3	05-06-12	21.86	2.20	2.01	4.05
4	06-06-12	22.235	1.72	1.53	2.34
5	07-06-12	22.11	-0.56	-0.75	0.56
6	08-06-12	22.12	0.05	-0.14	0.02
7	11-06-12	21.44	-3.07	-3.26	10.62
8	12-06-12	21.72	1.31	1.12	1.26
9	13-06-12	21.33	-1.80	-1.98	3.92
10	14-06-12	21.27	-0.28	-0.47	0.22
11	15-06-12	21.48	0.99	0.80	0.64
12	18-06-12	21.68	0.93	0.75	0.56
13	19-06-12	22.15	2.17	1.98	3.93
14	20-06-12	22.24	0.41	0.22	0.05
15	21-06-12	21.55	-3.10	-3.29	10.81
16	22-06-12	21.77	1.02	0.84	0.70
17	25-06-12	21.24	-2.43	-2.62	6.86
18	26-06-12	21.29	0.24	0.05	0.00
19	27-06-12	21.62	1.55	1.36	1.86
20	28-06-12	21.86	1.11	0.92	0.86
21	29-06-12	22.67	3.71	3.52	12.39
n = 21			$\sum x = 3.89$		$\sum(x - \bar{x})^2 = 67.77$

DESCRIPTIVE STATISTICS	
Mean $\left(\frac{\sum x}{n}\right)$	0.185223345
Median $\left(\frac{n+1}{2}\right)$	0.406320542
Standard Deviation $\left(\sqrt{variance}\right)$	0.153681617
Sample Variance $\left(\frac{\sum(x-\bar{x})2}{n}\right)$	3.227313961
Range	6.807915973
Minimum	-3.102517986
Maximum	3.705397987

4.13.1 JARQUE-BERA TEST:

JB (observed value)	0.721
JB (critical value)	5.991
DF	2
One-tailed p-value	0.697
Alpha	0.05

TEST INTERPRETATION:

H0: The variable from which the sample was extracted follows a Normal distribution.
Ha: The variable from which the sample was extracted does not follow a Normal distribution.
As the computed p-value is greater than the significance level alpha=0.05, one cannot reject the null hypothesis H0.
The risk to reject the null hypothesis H0 while it is true is 55.31%.

CRITICAL VALUE:

value of the statistic under the null hypothesis for the probability 1-alpha (right-tailed test)
reject the null hypothesis when the observed value is greater than the critical value

One - tailed p-value:

probability under the null hypothesis to obtain a result as extreme as the observed result, towards the right-tail of the distribution.
reject the null hypothesis when the probability is lower than the alpha level.

4.13.2 CONCLUSION:

At the level of significance Alpha=0.050 the decision is to not reject the null hypothesis that the sample follows a normal distribution.
In other words, the non-normality is not significant.

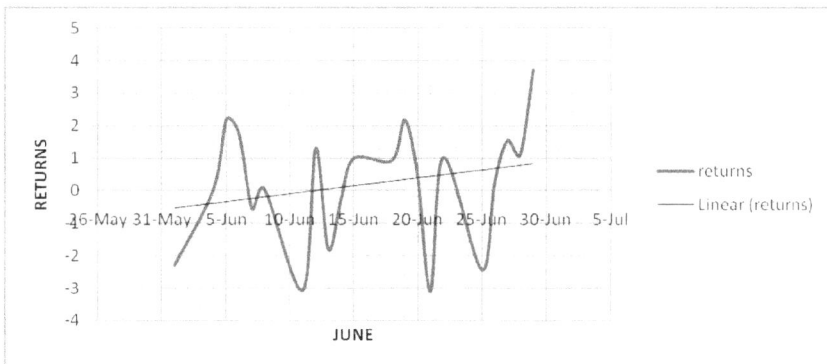

4.13.3 AUGMENTED DICKEY FULLER TEST RESULTS ON NASDAQ RETURNS FOR THE MONTH OF JUNE 2012

Null Hypothesis: NASDAQ RETURNS for the month of JUNE has a unit root
Exogenous: Constant
Lag Length: 1 (Fixed)

		t-Statistic	Prob.*
Augmented Dickey-Fuller test statistic		-2.288345	0.1852
Test critical values:	1% level	-3.831511	
	5% level	-3.029970	
	10% level	-2.655194	

*MacKinnon (1996) one-sided p-values.
NOTE: Probabilities and critical values calculated for 20 observations
and may not be accurate for a sample size of 19

Augmented Dickey-Fuller Test Equation
Dependent Variable: D(JUNE RETURNS)
Method: Least Squares

Sample (adjusted): 05/06/2012 - 29/06/2012
Included observations: 19 after adjustments

Variable	Coefficient	Std. Error	t-Statistic	Prob.
RETURNS05(-1)	-0.926596	0.404919	-2.288345	0.0361
D(RETURNS05(-1))	-0.097565	0.267604	-0.364589	0.7202
C	0.332499	0.448594	0.741202	0.4693

R-squared	0.466551	Mean dependent var	0.192632
Adjusted R-squared	0.399869	S.D. dependent var	2.515143
S.E. of regression	1.948433	Akaike info criterion	4.315867
Sum squared resid	60.74227	Schwarz criterion	4.464989
Log likelihood	-38.00074	Hannan-Quinn criter.	4.341105
F-statistic	6.996735	Durbin-Watson stat	1.695571
Prob(F-statistic)	0.006558		

The t-Statistic (-2.288345) is greater than the Critical Values at 1%, 5% and 10% significant levels (-3.831511, -3.029970 and -2.655194 respectively). Hence it is failed to reject the null hypothesis and it is concluded that the returns for the month of June 2012 are non-stationary.

4.14 RETURN, VARIANCE AND STANDARD DEVIATION OF NASDAQ FOR THE MONTH OF JULY – 2012

s.no	date	close	returns (x)	$(x - \bar{x})$	$(x - \bar{x})^2$
1	02-07-12	22.89	0.97	0.95	0.90
2	03-07-12	22.76	-0.57	-0.59	0.34
3	05-07-12	22.55	-0.92	-0.94	0.89
4	06-07-12	22.22	-1.46	-1.48	2.20
5	09-07-12	21.85	-1.67	-1.68	2.84
6	10-07-12	21.66	-0.87	-0.89	0.79
7	11-07-12	22.1	2.03	2.01	4.05
8	12-07-12	22.04	-0.27	-0.29	0.08
9	13-07-12	22.56	2.36	2.34	5.48
10	16-07-12	22.51	-0.22	-0.24	0.06
11	17-07-12	22.76	1.11	1.09	1.19
12	18-07-12	22.9	0.62	0.60	0.36
13	19-07-12	22.81	-0.39	-0.41	0.17
14	20-07-12	22.37	-1.93	-1.95	3.80
15	23-07-12	22.15	-0.98	-1.00	1.01
16	24-07-12	21.83	-1.44	-1.46	2.14
17	25-07-12	22.87	4.76	4.74	22.51
18	26-07-12	23.21	1.49	1.47	2.15
19	27-07-12	23.25	0.17	0.15	0.02
20	30-07-12	23.16	-0.39	-0.41	0.17
21	31-07-12	22.7	-1.99	-2.01	4.02
n = 21			$\sum x = 0.40$		$\sum(x - \bar{x})^2 = 55.17$

DESCRIPTIVE STATISTICS	
Mean $\left(\frac{\sum x}{n}\right)$	0.019271672
Median $\left(\frac{n+1}{2}\right)$	-0.387096774
Standard Deviation $\left(\sqrt{variance}\right)$	1.620802209
Sample Variance $\left(\frac{\sum(x-\bar{x})2}{n}\right)$	2.6269998
Range	6.750269194
Minimum	-1.986183074
Maximum	4.76408612

4.14.1 JARQUE-BERA TEST:

JB (observed value)	6.005
JB (critical value)	5.991
DF	2
One-tailed p-value	0.05
Alpha	0.05

TEST INTERPRETATION:

H0: The variable from which the sample was extracted follows a Normal distribution.
Ha: The variable from which the sample was extracted does not follow a Normal distribution.
As the computed p-value is equal to the significance level alpha=0.05, hence
the null hypothesis H0 is rejected.

CRITICAL VALUE:
value of the statistic under the null hypothesis for the probability 1-alpha (right-tailed test)
reject the null hypothesis when the observed value is greater than the critical value

One - tailed p-value:
probability under the null hypothesis to obtain a result as extreme as the observed result,
towards the right-tail of the distribution.
reject the null hypothesis when the probability is lower than the alpha level.

4.14.2   CONCLUSION:
At the level of significance Alpha=0.050 the decision is to reject the null hypothesis
that the sample follows a normal distribution.
In other words, the non-normality is significant.

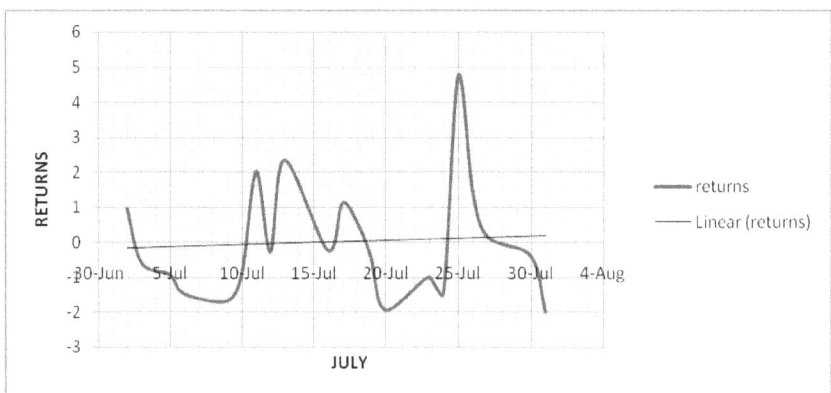

4.14.3 AUGMENTED DICKEY FULLER TEST RESULTS ON NASDAQ RETURNS FOR THE MONTH OF JULY 2012

Null Hypothesis: NASDAQ RETURNS for the month of JULY has a unit root
Exogenous: Constant
Lag Length: 1 (Fixed)

		t-Statistic	Prob.*
Augmented Dickey-Fuller test statistic		-2.448990	0.1427
Test critical values:	1% level	-3.831511	
	5% level	-3.029970	
	10% level	-2.655194	

*MacKinnon (1996) one-sided p-values.
NOTE: Probabilities and critical values calculated for 20 observations
and may not be accurate for a sample size of 19

Augmented Dickey-Fuller Test Equation
Dependent Variable: D(JULY RETURNS)
Method: Least Squares

Sample (adjusted): 04/07/2012 - 30/07/2012
Included observations: 19 after adjustments

Variable	Coefficient	Std. Error	t-Statistic	Prob.
RETURNS06(-1)	-0.835399	0.341120	-2.448990	0.0262
D(RETURNS06(-1))	-0.011541	0.256976	-0.044911	0.9647
C	-0.012688	0.418217	-0.030339	0.9762

R-squared	0.404957	Mean dependent var	-0.074737
Adjusted R-squared	0.330577	S.D. dependent var	2.217720
S.E. of regression	1.814500	Akaike info criterion	4.173437
Sum squared resid	52.67859	Schwarz criterion	4.322559
Log likelihood	-36.64765	Hannan-Quinn criter.	4.198674
F-statistic	5.444411	Durbin-Watson stat	1.929719
Prob(F-statistic)	0.015718		

The t-Statistic (-2.448990) is greater than the Critical Values at 1%, 5% and 10% significant levels (-3.831511, -3.029970 and -2.655194 respectively). Hence it is failed to reject the null hypothesis and it is concluded that the returns for the month of July 2012 are non-stationary.

4.15 CORRELATION TEST FOR THE RETURNS OF NSE AND NASDAQ FOR THE MONTH OF JANUARY 2012

S.No	Returns X (NSE)	X^2	Returns Y (NASDAQ)	Y^2	XY
1	-0.0743	0.01	1.84	3.39	-0.14
2	2.7724	7.69	-1.36	1.85	-3.77
3	-0.3284	0.11	0.16	0.03	-0.05
4	0.0063	0.00	-0.93	0.86	-0.01
5	0.0874	0.01	-0.41	0.17	-0.04
6	-0.1514	0.02	3.45	11.90	-0.52
7	-0.0864	0.01	-0.48	0.23	0.04
8	2.2508	5.07	-0.36	0.13	-0.81
9	0.2351	0.06	-0.64	0.41	-0.15
10	-0.611	0.37	-1.13	1.28	0.69
11	0.7193	0.52	1.06	1.12	0.76
12	0.1624	0.03	1.45	2.10	0.24
13	1.9163	3.67	0.8	0.64	1.53
14	-0.2315	0.05	0.47	0.22	-0.11
15	1.2632	1.60	0.79	0.62	1.00
16	0.6018	0.36	0.94	0.88	0.57
17	-0.0465	0.00	-0.27	0.07	0.01
18	1.6071	2.58	0.62	0.38	1.00
19	0.6036	0.36	-2.65	7.02	-1.60
20	0.8995	0.81	-2.13	4.54	-1.92
n = 20	$\sum X = 11.5957$	$\sum X^2 = 23.32$	$\sum Y = 1.22$	$\sum Y^2 = 37.85$	$\sum XY = -3.27$

$$\text{Correlation} = \frac{n\sum XY - \sum X \sum Y}{\sqrt{n\sum X^2 - (\sum X)^2}\sqrt{n\sum Y^2 - (\sum Y)^2}}$$

$$= \frac{20\times(-3.27) - (11.5957\times1.22)}{\sqrt{20\times23.32 - 11.5957^2}\sqrt{20\times37.85 - 1.22^2}}$$

$$= \frac{-65.4 - 14.146754}{18.2192\times27.4866}$$

$$= \frac{-79.5468}{500.7839}$$

$$= -0.159$$

4.15.1 PEARSON'S CORRELATION COEFFICIENT TEST (PARAMETRIC TEST):

Observed value	-0.159
Two-tailed p-value	0.503
Alpha	0.05

Two tailed p-value:

probability under the null hypothesis to obtain a result as extreme as the observed result, at the two tails of the distribution.

reject the null hypothesis when the probability is lower than the alpha level.

because the distrubution is symmetric, this probability is the double of the one-tailed p-value.

4.15.2 CONCLUSION:

At the level of significance Alpha=0.050 the decision is to not reject the null hypothesis of absence of correlation.

In other words, the correlation is not significant.

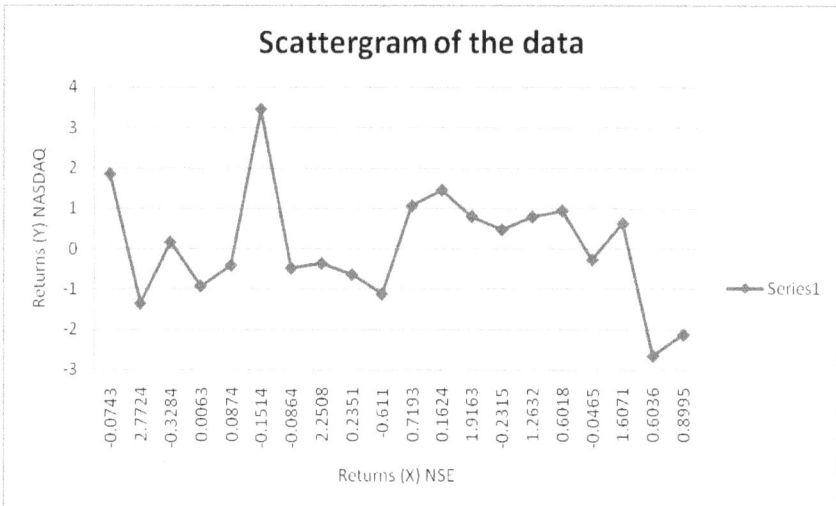

Scattergram of the data

4.16 CORRELATION TEST FOR THE RETURNS OF NSE AND NASDAQ FOR THE MONTH OF FEBRUARY 2012

S.No	Returns (X) NSE	X^2	Returns (Y) NASDAQ	Y^2	XY
1	0.72	0.5184	0.04	0.0016	0.0288
2	0.65	0.4225	-0.44	0.1936	-0.286
3	1.06	1.1236	1.66	2.7556	1.7596
4	0.67	0.4489	1.12	1.2544	0.7504
5	-0.49	0.2401	1.38	1.9044	-0.6762
6	0.62	0.3844	2.1	4.41	1.302
7	0.82	0.6724	-1.37	1.8769	-1.1234
8	-0.57	0.3249	0.46	0.2116	-0.2622
9	0.16	0.0256	1.38	1.9044	0.2208
10	0.48	0.2304	0	0	0
11	2.14	4.5796	-0.57	0.3249	-1.2198
12	-0.18	0.0324	2.06	4.2436	-0.3708
13	0.77	0.5929	0.22	0.0484	0.1694
14	0.77	0.5929	-0.78	0.6084	-0.6006
15	-1.82	3.3124	-1.43	2.0449	2.6026
16	-0.4	0.16	0.15	0.0225	-0.06
17	-0.98	0.9604	1.64	2.6896	-1.6072
18	-2.73	7.4529	0.37	0.1369	-1.0101
19	1.79	3.2041	-0.6	0.36	-1.074
20	0.18	0.0324	-1.09	1.1881	-0.1962
n=20	$\sum X = 3.66$	$\sum X^2 = 25.3112$	$\sum Y = 6.3$	$\sum Y^2 = 26.1798$	$\sum XY = -1.6529$

$$\text{Correlation} = \frac{n \sum XY - \sum X \sum Y}{\sqrt{n \sum X^2 - (\sum X)^2} \sqrt{n \sum Y^2 - (\sum Y)^2}}$$

$$= \frac{20 \times (-1.6529) - (3.66 \times 6.3)}{\sqrt{20 \times 25.3112 - 3.66^2} \sqrt{20 \times 26.1798 - 6.3^2}}$$

$$= \frac{-33.058 - 23.058}{22.1997 \times 21.99786}$$

$$= \frac{-56.116}{488.3459}$$

$$= -0.115$$

4.16.1 PEARSON'S CORRELATION COEFFICIENT TEST (PARAMETRIC TEST):

Observed value	-0.115
Two-tailed p-value	0.630
Alpha	0.05

Two tailed p-value:

probability under the null hypothesis to obtain a result as extreme as the observed result, at the two tails of the distribution.

reject the null hypothesis when the probability is lower than the alpha level.

because the distrubution is symmetric, this probability is the double of the one-tailed p-value.

4.16.2 CONCLUSION:

At the level of significance Alpha=0.050 the decision is to not reject the null hypothesis of absence of correlation.

In other words, the correlation is not significant.

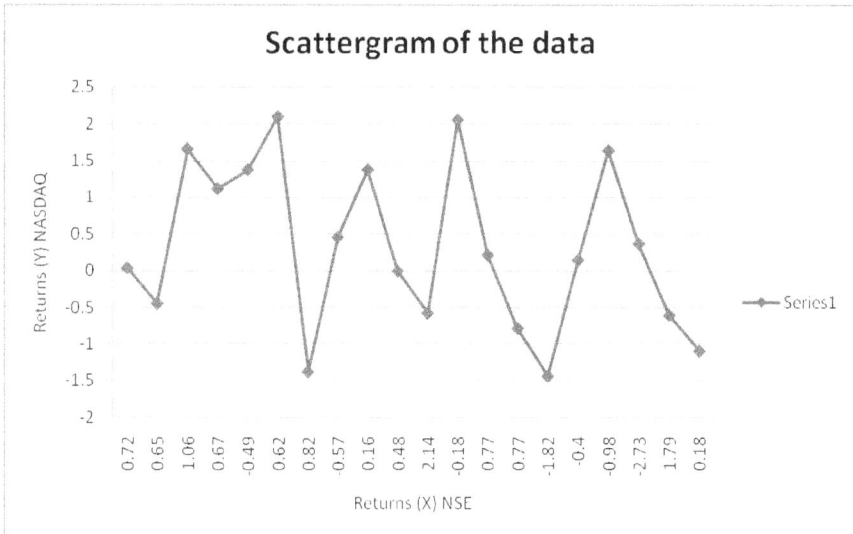

Scattergram of the data

4.17 CORRELATION TEST FOR THE RETURNS OF NSE AND NASDAQ FOR THE MONTH OF MARCH 2012

S.No	Returns (X) NSE	X^2	Returns (Y) NASDAQ	Y^2	XY
1	-0.49	0.2401	-0.11	0.0121	0.0539
2	0.37	0.1369	-0.76	0.5776	-0.2812
3	0	0	0.15	0.0225	0
4	-1.47	2.1609	-2.6	6.76	3.822
5	-1.1	1.21	0.67	0.4489	-0.737
6	-0.04	0.0016	1.21	1.4641	-0.0484
7	2.17	4.7089	0.69	0.4761	1.4973
8	0.49	0.2401	-1.11	1.2321	-0.5439
9	1.31	1.7161	3.41	11.6281	4.4671
10	0.63	0.3969	-0.86	0.7396	-0.5418
11	-1.53	2.3409	0.98	0.9604	-1.4994
12	-1.16	1.3456	-0.52	0.2704	0.6032
13	-1.14	1.2996	0.71	0.5041	-0.8094
14	0.34	0.1156	-0.3	0.09	-0.102
15	1.71	2.9241	0.49	0.2401	0.8379
16	-2.54	6.4516	0.11	0.0121	-0.2794
17	0.95	0.9025	-0.89	0.7921	-0.8455
18	-1.78	3.1684	2.03	4.1209	-3.6134
19	1.14	1.2996	-2.1	4.41	-2.394
20	-0.92	0.8464	-0.71	0.5041	0.6532
21	-0.31	0.0961	-2.27	5.1529	0.7037
22	2.25	5.0625	0.31	0.0961	0.6975
n=22	$\sum X = -1.12$	$\sum X^2 = 36.6644$	$\sum Y = -1.47$	$\sum Y^2 = 40.5143$	$\sum XY = 1.6404$

$$\text{Correlation} = \frac{n\sum XY - \sum X \sum Y}{\sqrt{n\sum X^2 - (\sum X)^2}\sqrt{n\sum Y^2 - (\sum Y)^2}}$$

$$= \frac{22 \times (1.6404) - (-1.12 \times -1.47)}{\sqrt{22 \times 36.6644 - (-1.12)^2}\sqrt{22 \times 40.5143 - (-1.47)^2}}$$

$$= \frac{36.0888 - 1.6464}{28.3789 \times 29.8186}$$

$$= \frac{34.4424}{846.2190}$$

$$= 0.041$$

4.17.1 PEARSON'S CORRELATION COEFFICIENT TEST (PARAMETRIC TEST):

Observed value	0.041
Two-tailed p-value	0.857
Alpha	0.05

Two tailed p-value:

probability under the null hypothesis to obtain a result as extreme as the observed result, at the two tails of the distribution.

reject the null hypothesis when the probability is lower than the alpha level.

because the distrubution is symmetric, this probability is the double of the one-tailed p-value.

4.17.2 CONCLUSION:

At the level of significance Alpha=0.050 the decision is to not reject the null hypothesis of absence of correlation.

In other words, the correlation is not significant.

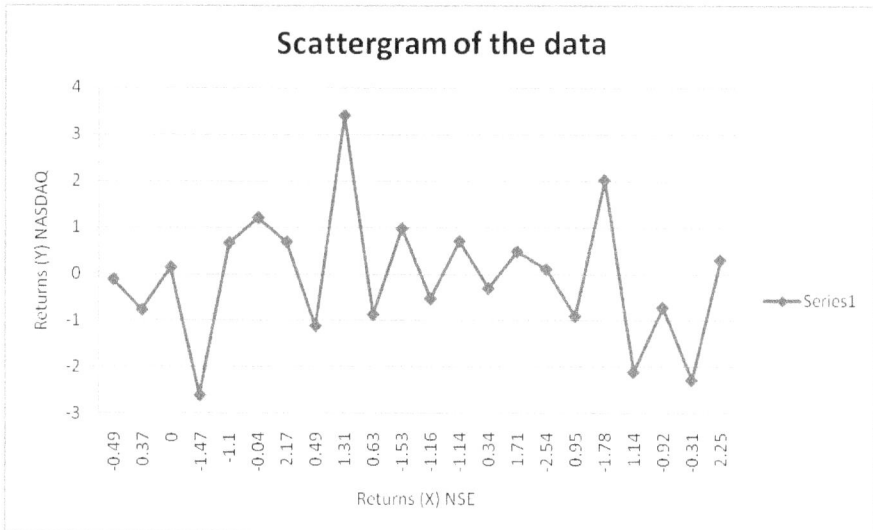

Scattergram of the data

4.18 CORRELATION TEST FOR THE RETURNS OF NSE AND NASDAQ FOR THE MONTH OF APRIL 2012

S.No	Returns (X) NSE	X^2	Returns (Y) NASDAQ	Y^2	XY
1	0.41	0.1681	0.12	0.0144	0.0492
2	0.76	0.5776	-0.77	0.5929	-0.5852
3	-0.66	0.4356	-1.98	3.9204	1.3068
4	-1.66	2.7556	1.19	1.4161	-1.9754
5	0.18	0.0324	-0.67	0.4489	-0.1206
6	-0.32	0.1024	-3	9	0.96
7	0.96	0.9216	0.57	0.3249	0.5472
8	-1.32	1.7424	0.89	0.7921	-1.1748
9	0.36	0.1296	-1.52	2.3104	-0.5472
10	1.22	1.4884	-0.57	0.3249	-0.6954
11	0.19	0.0361	1.43	2.0449	0.2717
12	0.61	0.3721	-0.28	0.0784	-0.1708
13	-0.78	0.6084	-0.04	0.0016	0.0312
14	-1.71	2.9241	1.38	1.9044	-2.3598
15	0.42	0.1764	-0.08	0.0064	-0.0336
16	-0.4	0.16	1.24	1.5376	-0.496
17	-0.25	0.0625	-0.83	0.6889	0.2075
18	0.03	0.0009	-0.2	0.04	-0.006
19	0.35	0.1225	0.28	0.0784	0.098
20	0.75	0.5625	-2.27	5.1529	-1.7025
n=20	$\sum X = -0.86$	$\sum X^2 = 13.3792$	$\sum Y = -5.11$	$\sum Y^2 = 30.6785$	$\sum XY = -6.3957$

$$\text{Correlation} = \frac{n\sum XY - \sum X \sum Y}{\sqrt{n\sum X^2 - (\sum X)^2}\sqrt{n\sum Y^2 - (\sum Y)^2}}$$

$$= \frac{20 \times (-6.3957) - (-0.86 \times -5.11)}{\sqrt{20 \times 13.3792 - (-0.86)^2}\sqrt{20 \times 30.6785 - (-5.11)^2}}$$

$$= \frac{-127.914 - 4.3946}{16.3354 \times 24.2375}$$

$$= \frac{-132.3086}{395.9293}$$

$$= -0.334$$

4.18.1 PEARSON'S CORRELATION COEFFICIENT TEST (PARAMETRIC TEST):

Observed value	-0.334
Two-tailed p-value	0.150
Alpha	0.05

Two tailed p-value:

probability under the null hypothesis to obtain a result as extreme as the observed result, at the two tails of the distribution.

reject the null hypothesis when the probability is lower than the alpha level.

because the distrubution is symmetric, this probability is the double of the one-tailed p-value.

4.18.2 CONCLUSION:

At the level of significance Alpha=0.050 the decision is to not reject the null hypothesis of absence of correlation.

In other words, the correlation is not significant.

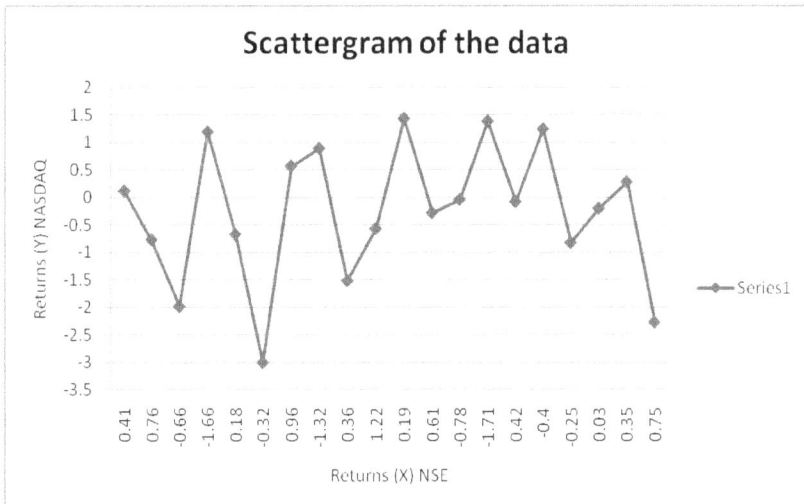

Scattergram of the data

4.19 CORRELATION TEST FOR THE RETURNS OF NSE AND NASDAQ FOR THE MONTH OF MAY 2012

S.No	Returns (X) NSE	X^2	Returns (Y) NASDAQ	Y^2	XY
1	-0.2883	0.083117	-0.53	0.2809	0.152799
2	-0.9687	0.93838	-1.43	2.0449	1.385241
3	-1.9573	3.831023	-1.74	3.0276	3.405702
4	0.5367	0.288047	0	0	0
5	-2.233	4.986289	-0.97	0.9409	2.16601
6	-0.503	0.253009	0.9	0.81	-0.4527
7	-0.1829	0.033452	1.73	2.9929	-0.31642
8	-0.7411	0.549229	-1.37	1.8769	1.015307
9	-0.4281	0.18327	-1.56	2.4336	0.667836
10	0.7132	0.508654	0.86	0.7396	0.613352
11	-1.7106	2.926152	0.51	0.2601	-0.87241
12	0.246	0.060516	-2.39	5.7121	-0.58794
13	0.4363	0.190358	-0.5	0.25	-0.21815
14	0.2985	0.089102	-4.39	19.2721	-1.31042
15	-0.9284	0.861927	3.59	12.8881	-3.33296
16	-0.5113	0.261428	-2.02	4.0804	1.032826
17	1.7733	3.144593	-2.28	5.1984	-4.04312
18	-0.0203	0.000412	-0.05	0.0025	0.001015
19	1.3261	1.758541	1.19	1.4161	1.578059
20	0.0893	0.007974	0.73	0.5329	0.065189
21	-0.7886	0.62189	-1.85	3.4225	1.45891
22	-0.5353	0.286546	0.32	0.1024	-0.1713
n=22	$\sum X = -6.3775$	$\sum X^2 = 21.86391$	$\sum Y = -11.25$	$\sum Y^2 = 68.2849$	$\sum XY = 2.236842$

$$\text{Correlation} = \frac{n\sum XY - \sum X \sum Y}{\sqrt{n\sum X^2 - (\sum X)^2}\sqrt{n\sum Y^2 - (\sum Y)^2}}$$

$$= \frac{22 \times (-2.236842) - (-6.3775 \times -11.25)}{\sqrt{22 \times 21.86391 - (-6.3775)^2}\sqrt{22 \times 68.2849 - (-11.25)^2}}$$

$$= \frac{-49.2105 - 71.746875}{20.984 \times 37.0905}$$

$$= \frac{-120.957}{778.3071}$$

$$= -0.155$$

4.19.1 PEARSON'S CORRELATION COEFFICIENT TEST (PARAMETRIC TEST):

Observed value	-0.029
Two-tailed p-value	0.898
Alpha	0.05

Two tailed p-value:

probability under the null hypothesis to obtain a result as extreme as the observed result, at the two tails of the distribution.

reject the null hypothesis when the probability is lower than the alpha level.

because the distrubution is symmetric, this probability is the double of the one-tailed p-value.

4.19.2 CONCLUSION:

At the level of significance Alpha=0.050 the decision is to not reject the null hypothesis of absence of correlation.

In other words, the correlation is not significant.

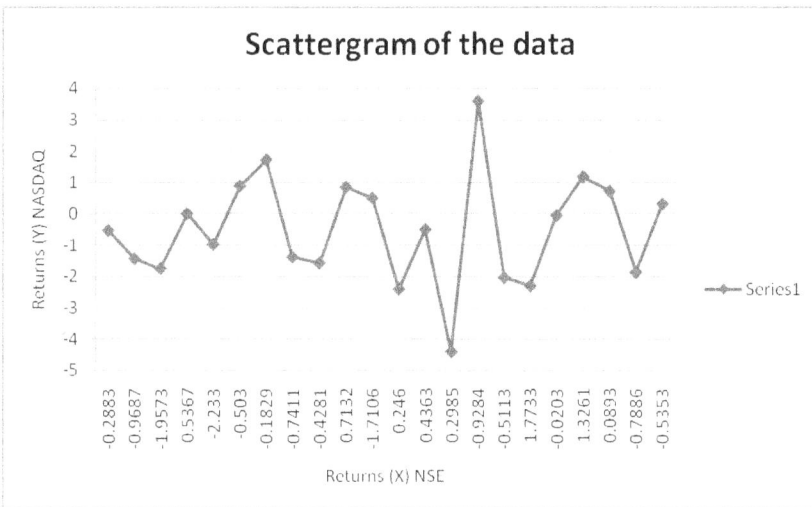

Scattergram of the data

4.20 CORRELATION TEST FOR THE RETURNS OF NSE AND NASDAQ FOR THE MONTH OF JUNE 2012

S.No	Returns (X) NSE	X^2	Returns (Y) NASDAQ	Y^2	XY
1	-1.4101	1.988382	-2.29	5.2441	3.229129
2	0.1353	0.018306	0.05	0.0025	0.006765
3	0.3125	0.097656	2.2	4.84	0.6875
4	2.7512	7.569101	1.72	2.9584	4.732064
5	1.0516	1.105863	-0.56	0.3136	-0.5889
6	0.3703	0.137122	0.05	0.0025	0.018515
7	-0.2812	0.079073	-3.07	9.4249	0.863284
8	1.2228	1.49524	1.31	1.7161	1.601868
9	0.1085	0.011772	-1.8	3.24	-0.1953
10	-1.3024	1.696246	-0.28	0.0784	0.364672
11	1.6677	2.781223	0.99	0.9801	1.651023
12	-1.4555	2.11848	0.93	0.8649	-1.35362
13	0.782	0.611524	2.17	4.7089	1.69694
14	0.3272	0.10706	0.41	0.1681	0.134152
15	0.8681	0.753598	-3.1	9.61	-2.69111
16	-0.3669	0.134616	1.02	1.0404	-0.37424
17	-0.6102	0.372344	-2.43	5.9049	1.482786
18	0.1202	0.014448	0.24	0.0576	0.028848
19	0.412	0.169744	1.55	2.4025	0.6386
20	0.141	0.019881	1.11	1.2321	0.15651
21	2.5198	6.349392	3.71	13.7641	9.348458
n=21	$\sum X = 7.3639$	$\sum X^2 = 27.63107$	$\sum Y = 3.93$	$\sum Y^2 = 68.5541$	$\sum XY = 21.43796$

$$\text{Correlation} = \frac{n\sum XY - \sum X \sum Y}{\sqrt{n\sum X^2 - (\sum X)^2}\sqrt{n\sum Y^2 - (\sum Y)^2}}$$

$$= \frac{21 \times 21.43796 - (7.3639 \times 3.93)}{\sqrt{21 \times 27.63107 - 7.3639^2}\sqrt{21 \times 68.5541 - 3.93^2}}$$

$$= \frac{450.197 - 28.96134}{22.9352 \times 37.7384}$$

$$= \frac{421.23566}{865.53775}$$

$$= \mathbf{0.487}$$

4.20.1 PEARSON'S CORRELATION COEFFICIENT TEST (PARAMETRIC TEST):

Observed value	0.487
Two-tailed p-value	0.025
Alpha	0.05

Two tailed p-value:

probability under the null hypothesis to obtain a result as extreme as the observed result, at the two tails of the distribution.

reject the null hypothesis when the probability is lower than the alpha level.

because the distrubution is symmetric, this probability is the double of the one-tailed p-value.

4.20.2 CONCLUSION:

At the level of significance Alpha=0.050 the decision is to reject the null hypothesis of absence of correlation.

In other words, the correlation is significant.

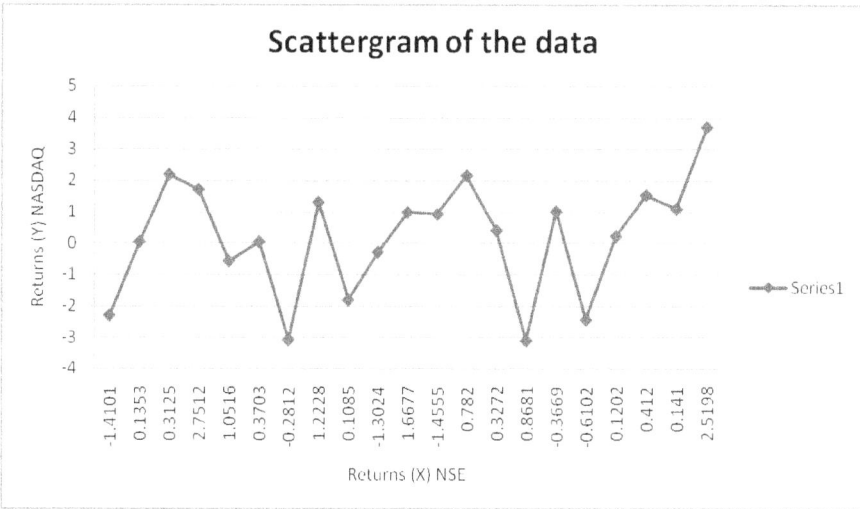

Scattergram of the data

4.21 CORRELATION TEST FOR THE RETURNS OF NSE AND NASDAQ FOR THE MONTH OF JULY 2012

S.No	Returns (X) NSE	X^2	Returns (Y) NASDAQ	Y^2	XY
1	-0.0994	0.00988	0.97	0.9409	-0.09642
2	0.1771	0.031364	-0.57	0.3249	-0.10095
3	0.2761	0.076231	-0.92	0.8464	-0.25401
4	0.4668	0.217902	-1.46	2.1316	-0.68153
5	-0.1943	0.037752	-1.67	2.7889	0.324481
6	-0.7862	0.61811	-0.87	0.7569	0.683994
7	1.3308	1.771029	2.03	4.1209	2.701524
8	-0.7305	0.53363	-0.27	0.0729	0.197235
9	-1.339	1.792921	2.36	5.5696	-3.16004
10	-0.1528	0.023348	-0.22	0.0484	0.033616
11	-0.5739	0.329361	1.11	1.2321	-0.63703
12	-0.0847	0.007174	0.62	0.3844	-0.05251
13	0.4516	0.203943	-0.39	0.1521	-0.17612
14	0.5061	0.256137	-1.93	3.7249	-0.97677
15	-0.7172	0.514376	-0.98	0.9604	0.702856
16	-1.6743	2.80328	-1.44	2.0736	2.410992
17	0.2003	0.04012	4.76	22.6576	0.953428
18	-0.3627	0.131551	1.49	2.2201	-0.54042
19	-1.3034	1.698852	0.17	0.0289	-0.22158
20	1.1273	1.270805	-0.39	0.1521	-0.43965
21	1.9599	3.841208	-1.99	3.9601	-3.9002
n=21	$\sum X = -1.5224$	$\sum X^2 = 16.20898$	$\sum Y = 0.41$	$\sum Y^2 = 55.1477$	$\sum XY = -3.22911$

$$\textbf{Correlation} \ = \ \frac{n\sum XY - \sum X \sum Y}{\sqrt{n\sum X^2 - (\sum X)^2}\sqrt{n\sum Y^2 - (\sum Y)^2}}$$

$$= \frac{21 \times (-3.22911) - (-1.5224 \times 0.41)}{\sqrt{21 \times 16.20898 - (-1.5224)^2}\sqrt{21 \times 55.1477 - 0.41^2}}$$

$$= \frac{-67.811 + 0.624184}{18.3867 \times 34.0284}$$

$$= \frac{-67.186816}{625.6700}$$

$$= -0.107$$

4.21.1 PEARSON'S CORRELATION COEFFICIENT TEST (PARAMETRIC TEST):

Observed value	-0.107
Two-tailed p-value	0.643
Alpha	0.05

Two tailed p-value:

probability under the null hypothesis to obtain a result as extreme as the observed result, at the two tails of the distribution.

reject the null hypothesis when the probability is lower than the alpha level.

because the distrubution is symmetric, this probability is the double of the one-tailed p-value.

4.21.2 CONCLUSION:

At the level of significance Alpha=0.050 the decision is to not reject the null hypothesis of absence of correlation.

In other words, the correlation is not significant.

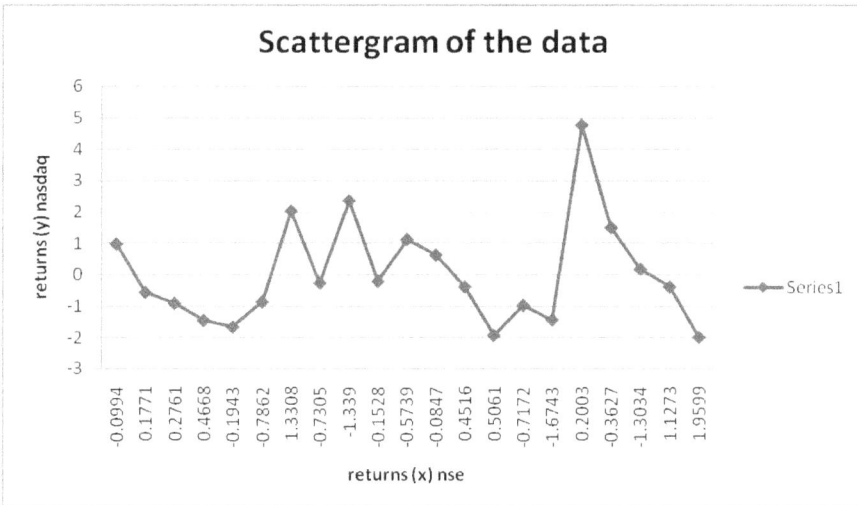

Scattergram of the data

CHAPTER – V

CONCLUSIONS

5.1   DATA ANALYSIS

As outlined in the methodology, the analysis of the data was conducted in four steps.

First, correlation has been calculated between the returns of NSE and NASDAQ. In the month of June and March the correlation between BSE SENSEX and NASDAQ is 0.49 and 0.04 respectively. So there exist slight positive relationship and all data points are form as non linear structure and tilts upwards towards right. Remaining all the months there exist low correlation, and in the months of January and April there exists negative correlation i.e.
-0.16 and -0.33, so there exists strong negative relationship and all data points tilts downward towards right.

Second, Normality test was applied on both the series to determine the nature of their distributions. For this purpose, Jarque-Bera statistics were computed, which are shown in Table 2 and Table 5 along with DESCRIPTIVE STATISTICS for the two series. Skewness value 0 and kurtosis value 3 indicate that the variables are normally distributed. The skewness coefficient, in excess of unity is taken to be fairly extreme [Chou 1969]. High or low kurtosis value indicates extreme leptokurtic or extreme platykurtic [Parkinson 1987]. From the obtained statistics, it is evident that both the variables are non-normally distributed, as the skewness values for Nifty returns and NASDAQ returns are--0.295287 and 0.297429 respectively and the kurtosis values are 4.712687 and 9.096539 respectively.

Third, having affirmed the non-normal distribution of the two variables, the question of stationarity of the two time series posed concerns. Simplest way to check for stationarity is to plot time series graph and observe the trends in mean, variance and autocorrelation. A time series is said to be stationary if its mean and variance are constant over time. The line plots for the two series (log normal value of relatives) are shown in Fig 1.1 and Fig1.2 respectively. As seen in the plots, for both the series, the mean and variance appear to be constant as the plot rends neither upward nor downward. At the same time, the vertical fluctuations also indicate that the variance, too, is not changing. This hints that stationarity in both the series in their level forms.

Since in addition to visual inspection, formal econometric tests are also needed to unambiguously decide the actual nature of time series, ADF test was performed to check the stationarity of the time series. The results are shown in Table 3 and Table 6.

Comparing the obtained ADF statistics for the two variables with the critical values for rejection of hypothesis of existence of unit root, it becomes evident that the obtained statistics for NSE returns and NASDAQ returns, fall above the critical values at 1%, 5%, and 10% significance levels except in the month of April and may for NASDAQ and January and July for NSE; thereby, leading to the rejection of the hypothesis of unit root for both the series. Hence, it can be safely concluded on the basis of ADF test statistics that returns of both NSE and NASDAQ for the period of January 2012 to July 2012 found to be non-stationary at level form.

5.2   SCOPE FOR FURTHER RESEARCH

First, we have limited our study to only the returns of National Stock Exchange in India and NASDAQ in USA. Needless to say, we must exercise caution in generalizing to other exchange rate and stock returns.

Second, the same can be said regarding the performance measures used. We have restricted our attention to only four performance measures. The findings may change if other performance measures are used.

Third, we have also considered only one-step-ahead forecasting. Multi-step-ahead forecasting could yield different results.

Fourth, we have not used any other exogenous variable and have used only past returns as inputs.

Finally, we have been limited by the software we have used. We have had to use fairly primitive software i.e. Eviews7. We hope to bring all this into our further. The other fruitful areas for further research are the following.

1) First, is to combine methodology of linear models. It is suspected that most time series contain a linear trend and a nonlinear component. Hence, a combination approach in which linear model captures linear patterns and nonlinear patterns is expected to produce even better results than linear model used singly.

2) Second the study can be further carried from normality test to Granger causality and then to application of GARCH models to examine the co-movement and volatility transmission between US and Indian stock markets. It is found that the simple ARMAGARCH model performs better than the more complex Two-stage GARCH model. Two- stage GARCH model and a simple univariate ARMA-GARCH model can be applied to capture the mechanism by which NASDAQ Composite daytime returns and volatility have an impact on not only the conditional returns but also on the conditional volatility of Nifty overnight returns. This we hope to do in our further research.

3) Third, the robustness of networks to the changing structures, or turning points typically associated with exchange rates and stock prices can be investigated in further research by using multiple training and test samples systematically chosen from the original series. Fourth and finally, we have only used past returns as inputs to the network. However, technical trading rules can be profitably used in the set of inputs to the network to make more accurate forecast of exchange rate and stock returns.

5.3   CONCLUSION

We investigate the short run dynamic inter linkages between the US and Indian stock markets, using daytime and overnight returns of NSE Nifty and NASDAQ Composite from 1st January2012 to 31stJuly 2012. This approach provides an explicit, empirically based; quantitative description of the way information propagates from NASDAQ and is being incorporated by NSE overnight returns. The main findings are as follows:

The coefficient of correlation between the two variables was computed, which indicated slight negative correlation between them. There is an overall negative as well as positive correlation of returns between the NSE and NASDAQ, because out of (7) month data collected (5) months have negative correlation and (2) months have positive correlation on returns.

Application of Jarque-Bera test yielded statistics that affirmed non-normal distribution of both the variables. This posed questions on the stationarity of the two series. Hence subsequently, stationarity of the two series was checked with ADF test and the results showed non stationarity at level forms for both the series. This made way for determining the direction of influence between the two variables.

The previous day's daytime returns of both NASDAQ Composite and NSE Nifty have significant impact on the NSE Nifty overnight return of the following day. However, the volatility spillover effects are significant only from NASDAQ Composite implying that the conditional volatility of Nifty overnight returns is imported from US. We found that the effect of NASDAQ daytime return volatility shocks, on average, is 9.51% and that of Nifty daytime return volatility is a mere 0.5%. Turning to out of sample forecasts however, we found that by including the information revealed by NASDAQ day trading provides better forecasts of mean levels of Nifty overnight returns but does not significantly improve the prediction of volatility. At foremost interest in much of the empirical international financial literature is to study the extent to which markets have become internationally integrated. Insights into information flows in markets will increase the understanding of the relevant mechanisms at work during extreme situations such as market crashes, which in turn can provide guidelines for intervention and tax policies. This study contributes in a modest manner with reference to Indian stock market integration with the US stock market. The results reported are in tune with the previous studies, which have examined the co-movement of Indian markets with other markets and suggested a very low degree of correlation. Since the correlations across the stock markets are time-varying it can be concluded that NSE is not correlated with NASDAQ for the study period between January 2012 to July 2012.

However in the long run there is strong evidence that NSE Nifty is in tune with NASDAQ Composite over the sample period. Various explanations can be offered for this phenomenon and these range from
(I) Deregulation of Indian financial market since 1992, including increased efforts to implement liberalization measures.
(II) Increase in macroeconomic policy coordination,
(III) Expanding influence of multinational corporations,
(IV) Increased participation of FIIs in Indian stock market.
(V) Increasing international cross-listing of Indian firms in US markets and
(VI) Transmitted from one market to the other.

REFERENCES

Angela Ng (2000), *"Volatility spillover effects from Japan and the US to the Pacific-Basin,"* Journal ofInternational Money and Finance, 19, pp 207-233.

Becker, K. G., Finnerty, J. E. & Manoj Gupta (1990), *"The Intertemporal Relation Between the US &Japanese Stock Markets,"* Journal of Finance, 45, pp1297-1306

Engle, R.F. and V. Ng. (1993), "*Measuring and Testing the Impact of News on Volatility,*" The Journal ofFinance, 48, 1749-1778.

Engle R. F.. and Andrew J. Patton (2000), *"What Good is A Volatility Model?,"* Quantitative Finance, Volume 1 (2001) 237–245.

Eun, C. & Shim, S. (1989), *"International Transmission of Stock Market Movements,"* JFQA, 24, pp241-256.

Cheung & Lilian K. Ng (1992), *"Interactions Between the U. S. and Japan Stock Market Indices,"* Jl. OfInternational Financial Markets, Institutions & Money, Vol 2(2), pp51-70

Granger, Clive W.J. (1969), *"Investigating Causal Relations by Econometric Models and Cross SpectralMethods,"* Econometrica,37 pp 424-438.

Hamao, Y., Masulis, R., and Ng, V. (1990) *"Correlations in Price Changes and Volatility acrossInternational Stock Markets,"* Review of Financial Studies, 3, 281-307.

Hilliard, J. (1979), *"The Relationship between Equity Indices on World Exchanges"* Journal of Finance, 34(1), pp 103-117.

John Wei, K.C., Yu-Jane Liu, Yang & Chaung (1995), *"Volatility and price change spillover effects across the developed and emerging markets,"* Pacific-Basin FinanceJournal, Vol 3, pp 113-136.

Kee-Hong Bae, Karolyi (1994), *"Good news, bad news and international spillovers of stock return volatilitybetween Japan and the US,"* Pacific-Basin Finance Jl.,2, 405-438.

King, M. A. and S. Wadhwani (1990), *"Transmission of Volatility between Stock Markets,"* Review ofFinancial Studies, 3, pp 5-33.

King, M., Sentana, E. & Wadhwani, S. (1994),"*Volatility and Links between national markets*,"Econometrica, 62(4), pp901-933.

Koch, P. & Koch, R.(1991), "*Evolution in Dynamic Linkages Across Daily National Stock Indexes*,"Journal of International Money and Finance, 10, pp231-251.

Koutmos, G. (1999), "*Asymmetric price & volatility adjustments in emerging Asian stock markets,*" Journal ofBusiness Finance & Accounting, 26, (1)&(2), pp83-101.

Lin, Engle & Ito (1994), "*Do Bulls or Bears Move Across Borders? International Transmissions of StockReturns and Volatility,*" Review of Financial Studies,7,pp507-538

ONLINE SOURCES

1. Wikipedia: www.wikipedia.org
2. NSE india: www.nseindia.com
3. NASDAQ: www.nasdaq.com

ANNEXURE – FIGURES AND TABLES

Fig 1 : RETURNS FOR THE PERIOD JANUARY 2012 TO JULY 2012

FIG 1.1 : MONTHLYRETURNS OF NASDAQ

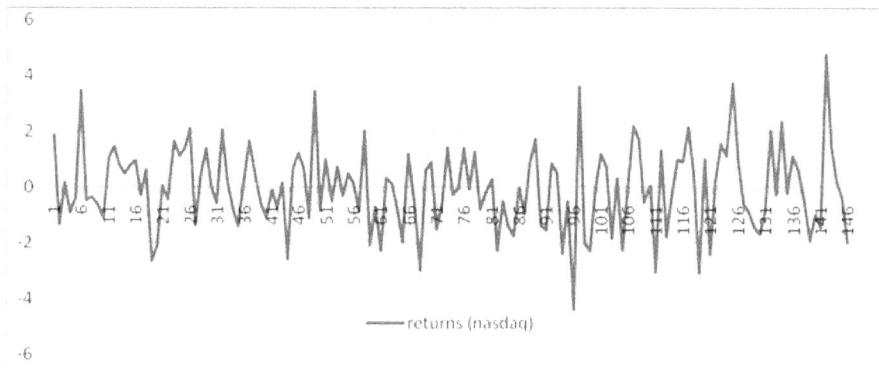

returns (nasdaq)

FIG 1.2 : MONTHLY RETURNS OF NSE NIFTY

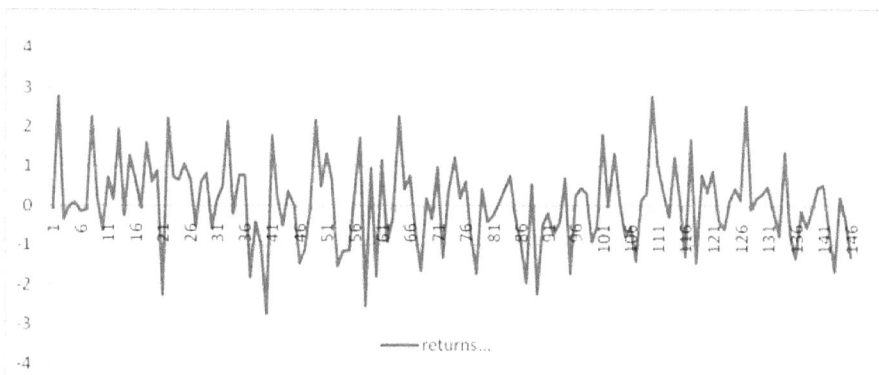

returns...

FIG 2 : MARKET TRADING HOURS

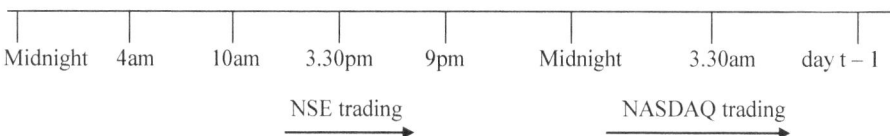

Midnight   4am   10am   3.30pm   9pm   Midnight   3.30am   day t – 1

NSE trading   NASDAQ trading

Table 1 : DESCRIPTIVE STATISTICS of NASDAQ for the period January 2012 to July 2012

Statistic	January	February	March	April	May	June	July
No. of observations	20	20	22	20	22	21	21
Minimum	-2.655	-1.429	-2.600	-2.998	-4.391	-3.103	-1.986
Maximum	3.453	2.101	3.406	1.433	3.593	3.705	4.764
Range	6.107	3.530	6.006	4.431	7.984	6.808	6.750
Median	-0.054	0.188	-0.001	-0.139	-0.513	0.406	-0.387
Mean	0.060	0.316	-0.067	-0.256	-0.511	0.185	0.019
Variance (n)	1.891	1.211	1.836	1.468	2.844	3.227	2.627
Standard deviation (n)	1.375	1.100	1.355	1.211	1.686	1.796	1.621
Skewness (Pearson)	0.254	0.095	0.322	-0.522	0.129	-0.346	1.160
Kurtosis (Pearson)	0.263	-1.187	0.425	-0.412	0.322	-0.588	1.215
Mean absolute deviation	1.097	0.934	1.046	0.959	1.355	1.439	1.272

Table 2 : Jarque-Bera Test Results of NASDAQ for the period January 2012 to July 2012

Statistic	January	February	March	April	May	June	July
JB (observed value)	0.272	1.204	0.546	1.049	0.156	0.721	6.005
JB (critical value)	5.991	5.991	5.991	5.991	5.991	5.991	5.991
DF	2	2	2	2	2	2	2
p-value	0.873	0.548	0.761	0.592	0.925	0.697	0.05
Alpha	0.05	0.05	0.05	0.05	0.05	0.05	0.05

Table 3 : Augmented Dickey – Fuller (ADF) Test Results of NASDAQ for the period January 2012 to July 2012

Statistic	January	February	March	April	May	June	July
ADF test statistic	-1.8072	-3.7652	-2.6546	-4.3394	-4.3308	-2.2883	-2.4490
Critical values : 1% level	-3.9203	-3.8574	-3.8085	-3.8574	-3.8085	-3.8315	-3.8315
5% level	-3.0656	-3.0404	-3.0207	-3.0404	-3.0207	-3.0299	-3.0299
10% level	-2.6735	-2.6606	-2.6564	-2.6606	-2.6504	-2.6552	-2.6552

Table 4 : DESCRIPTIVE STATISTICS of NSE for the period January 2012 to July 2012

Statistic	January	February	March	April	May	June	July
No. of observations	22	20	22	20	22	21	22
Minimum	-2.256	-2.728	-2.544	-1.706	-2.233	-1.456	-1.674
Maximum	2.772	2.140	2.253	1.215	1.773	2.751	1.960
Range	5.028	4.868	4.798	2.921	4.006	4.207	3.634
Median	0.199	0.549	-0.018	0.185	-0.358	0.312	-0.092
Mean	0.525	0.183	-0.052	-0.042	-0.290	0.351	-0.044
Variance (n)	1.236	1.231	1.665	0.666	0.910	1.193	0.749

Standard deviation (n)	1.112	1.110	1.290	0.816	0.954	1.092	0.866
Skewness (Pearson)	0.013	-0.797	0.065	-0.644	-0.014	0.370	0.225
Kurtosis (Pearson)	0.294	0.720	-0.869	-0.488	-0.063	-0.045	-0.153
Mean absolute deviation	0.872	0.848	1.085	0.675	0.738	0.809	0.681

Table 5 : Jarque-Bera Test Results of NSE for the period January 2012 to July 2012

Statistic	January	February	March	April	May	June	July
JB (observed value)	0.08	2.552	0.707	1.582	0.004	0.481	0.207
JB (critical value)	5.991	5.991	5.991	5.991	5.991	5.991	5.991
DF	2	2	2	2	2	2	2
p-value	0.961	0.279	0.702	0.453	0.998	0.786	0.902
Alpha	0.05	0.05	0.05	0.05	0.05	0.05	0.05

Table 6 : Augmented Dickey – Fuller (ADF) Test Results of NSE for the period Januray 2012 to July 2012

Statistic	January	February	March	April	May	June	July
ADF test statistic	-4.4517	-2.6472	-2.8083	-3.4294	-2.7380	-2.9062	-3.6977
Critical values : 1% level	-3.8085	-3.8574	-3.8085	-3.3574	-3.8085	-3.8315	-3.6085
5% level	-3.0206	-3.0404	-3.0207	-3.0404	-3.0206	-3.0299	-3.0206
10% level	-2.6504	-2.6605	-2.8504	-2.6606	-2.7504	-2.9552	-2.6504

Table 7 : Summary of Correlation between NSE Nifty and NASDAQ for the period January 2012 to July 2012

Statistic	January	February	March	April	May	June	July
no.observations	20	20	22	20	22	21	21
correlation	-0.159	-0.115	0.041	-0.334	-0.029	0.487	-0.107
p-value	0.503	0.63	0.857	0.15	0.898	0.025	0.643
coefficient of determination R^2	0.025	0.013	0.002	0.112	0.001	0.237	0.012

.

www.ingramcontent.com/pod-product-compliance
Lightning Source LLC
Chambersburg PA
CBHW060628210326
41520CB00010B/1520